Darlene's story carries you along, opening to the reader a world of poverty in West Louisville, and reveals how she rose above her circumstances. Throughout her life, the longing for a love that was real led her eventually to the Source. This book is a window to her journey. Read and be blessed.

> – Betty Allen

When Darlene was in elementary school, she and her three brothers and two sisters had the courage to come to church by themselves, a bit thrown together; we could only imagine the struggles and effort it took for them to get there. None of us knew the secret she was carrying or the pain in her heart until many years later. In this story, she shares, experience by experience, how God has brought healing to her life. Darlene writes with transparency that draws you in and touches your heart.

> – Linda Allen

About the Author

Darlene Snow lives in Crestwood, Kentucky with her husband and two of their four children. She had the honor of teaching children with the Pre-Kindergarten program of Jefferson County Public Schools for the past twenty years. Darlene is a *Social Butterfly for Jesus* who spreads words of love and hope.

Contact Info:

Darlene Snow

P.O. Box 453

Crestwood, KY 40014

darlene.snow@outlook.com

http://www.facebook.com/AGirlNamedDarlene

A GIRL NAMED DARLENE

A Journey from Abuse
to Healing

by

Darlene Snow

Author photograph © Renae Wease
Cover design by Steve Snow
Editor by Lorena Lasky

To Renae and Michael

Thanks for being the reason
I would go to bed in the evenings
and get up in the mornings.
Love, Mom

Acknowledgements

This book could not have been written if it were not for God. I give God all the Praise and Glory for always being with me as a child, teen, and still today as an adult.

There are so many people who came into my life to help me at certain times. There is no way I can name each and every one. There are a few I will mention:

My children, Renae and Michael, who gave me unconditional love; then Nathaniel and Nicholas who allowed me to be their mother.

My mentor, Dr. Rosie Young, who believed in me and opened doors to allow me to work with children. Dr. Young went above and beyond as a principal for our students and staff at Watson Lane Elementary.

The Allen's who were a major part during my earlier years. Even though I went to Portland Christian Church, Mrs. Allen taught me about God and also gave me cooking skills. Without her even knowing, Ms. Allen got me through the worst day of my life.

My childhood friends Sheila Sayre Mullins, Dawn Sallee, Missy Devine, and Leona Oller who have been friends for life. We don't get to see each other very often, but we know that we are there for one another.

My co-workers, Ms. Michelle and Ms. Pat, who let me vent about the good and the bad things going on in my life. Ms. Michelle and Ms. Pat always gave me advice—and sometimes even great advice—when I asked. Most of the time, however, I didn't follow their advice, but they were both great listeners.

There are not enough words to describe the thanks I have for Terry Young and my adoptive family Glenn, Joyce, Connie, Doug, Kim, Dean, Tonya, Rick, Michael, Debra, Vic, Diane, and many others who are part of my extended family. They made a huge difference in my life and showed me what a "real family" was like.

A very special thanks to WDRB and to Lindsay Allen for doing a story on the hidden hero, Leslie Thomas, co-founder of SOAR (Survivors of Abuse Restored). SOAR has given me the tools I need to heal and set me on a journey of recovery.

I also want to give thanks and recognition to the AAUW (America Association of University Woman) Morehead State University, Space Science Center and SpaceTrek.

To help with my grammar issues, my first editor was Mae. I am so thankful that God put Mae in my life to assist me and make corrections in my story until God put in place who He wants to be the editor of my book. After much praying about what to do with my book, I knew I needed an editor that was knowledgeable about references and how to format my book. I am honored and blessed to have Lorena Lasky who wanted to be my editor.

Even on my worst days, I still forget sometimes that God has a plan for me. I didn't need what I thought was the most "Amazing Man" to love me. God showed me that having a simple man is worth more than gold. The man I thank God for is Steve Snow. I simply cannot find the words that would give you an accurate glimpse of how much unconditional love Steve has given me. He lets me be me. Even on my worst days, Steve still loves me. I am honored and blessed to have Steve as my husband.

CONTENTS

Prologue   ix

Chapter 1: Poor in Portland   1

Chapter 2: Abused as a Child   8

Chapter 3: Raped as a Teen   15

Chapter 4: Moving Out at the Age of 15   42

Chapter 5: Returning to Louisville   51

Chapter 6: Getting Married   53

Chapter 7: Having Children   59

Chapter 8: Controlled   79

Chapter 9: Getting Divorced   86

Chapter 10: The Man of my Dreams   97

Chapter 11: Dating my Ex   105

Chapter 12: Adoptive Family   113

Contents

Chapter 13: College   119

Chapter 14: Brain Tumor   125

Chapter 15: House Fire   142

Chapter 16: Reflections   151

Chapter 17: Too Good to be True   159

Chapter 18: Forgiveness   184

Chapter 19: I Kept on Believing   187

Chapter 20: SHACK   189

Chapter 21: Never Say Never   192

Chapter 22: Growing in Love   208

Chapter 23: Anger and Depression   213

Epilogue: Mother and Me   219

Glossary of Characters   242

SOAR Information   246

Other Resources   247

PROLOGUE

It seems like all my life I have been on a journey. The journey I have been on was to find love. I wanted, needed and desired to be loved. I felt there was a hole in my body that just couldn't be filled. I was missing something. Was it the lack of love and protection from my mother? Was it because I didn't have a father?

Give thanks to the Lord, for he is good.
His love endures forever. ~ Psalm 136:1

I know God loves me forever. I also know I don't need anything or anyone in my life except for God. However, as a child, teen and adult, I wanted to feel loved.

As you read my story, you will see me being on mountain tops and down in the valleys. The mountain tops happened when I felt loved but most of the time it was short-lived or I found love in the wrong places.

Sometimes the valleys were hard to climb out of because of depression and feeling unworthy of love. It is also where I found God was with me every step I took no matter how bad life gets and I would grow closer to God. Sometimes the valleys were more of a safe place for me.

My story is to help someone know there is hope and that there are people who love them. Sometimes those people are right in front of you.

My story is also about bringing to light the statistics that 1 out of 3 women and 1 out of 5 men have been sexually abused as a child. In the past, I blamed myself for being abused. I thought I must have been doing something wrong and was being punished by God.

Walk with me on my journey to find love, heal from my abuse, and discover who is the main source of my healing.

CHAPTER 1

Poor in Portland

My early years of being a child were just okay. I really didn't know I was poor. Sure, I noticed that the other children would come to school with nicer clothes on or that their parents would bring them to school, but I really didn't think I was poor.

It wasn't until my childhood friend Sheila told me I was poor that I began to have this awareness. We were sitting in the cafeteria of Dolfinger Elementary when she asked me, "How does it feel to be poor?" I replied, "I don't know, because I am not poor." Then she listed the facts that made me realize I was indeed poor. In no way did she tell me this in malice. At that time, I think she started taking care of me. She would share her lunch with me. She wouldn't let anyone pick on me, and one time she went home and told her mom that a teacher hit me in the middle of my back. Well, to say the least, her mom came to school and talked to the principal about what

Sheila saw. They asked me about it and I told them that I must have done something wrong, something the teacher didn't like. They asked me if I told my parents. I told them I only had a mother, I didn't know who my father was, and my mother was doing the best she could. So, I didn't tell my mother because I didn't want her to worry about me. However, the real truth is that I didn't tell her because if she thought I did something wrong, I would be in even more trouble.

It was good to have Sheila as my friend. But I wished I could have told her my secret. I would have just liked to tell someone so they could tell me what I did to God to make Him so mad at me.

There are some good memories of my childhood. A special memory is when my Aunt Hazel and Uncle Dick came down from Indianapolis and my mother would be proud of me because I would sing and dance for them. No, I am neither a singer nor a dancer, but as a child I could entertain. I loved that I got to stay up late and dance for them. They would put me on the kitchen table and turn on the radio. I would sing and dance my heart out. I wanted the attention then because I never knew when I would get a kind word or hug.

When Aunt Hazel and Uncle Dick came to visit, we didn't have to worry about food. They must have known we were poor, because they would either bring food with them or they would go to the store and buy lots of food. Then Aunt Hazel and my Aunt Mildred would cook for us. I was sad that the visits were few and far between. Standing on a kitchen table singing and dancing is one of my happiest memories. It was as though I was storing up positive things to keep me going in the bad times.

I later learned that when you are poor, you move a lot. My mother had six children and lived on welfare. I hated moving because you would meet friends and then you would move again. We didn't stay in a house for very long. I think my favorite house that we lived in for a short time was a house in Portland. It had an upstairs and a huge bathroom that had little closets. I found out later that they were dressing rooms. They were a great place to hide and stay safe. The only thing is that you had to be upstairs before anyone saw you, because the steps would give you away.

I have two sisters, Linda and Tina, and we had to sleep in the same bed. I didn't mind, though, because I wasn't afraid when they slept with me. I wished I could say that everything was peaches and cream, but it wasn't.

I have three brothers—Paul, Terry and Larry—who also had to share a bed. I know now that, in most cases, this is not normal. Being poor and having a big family means you do things differently.

I didn't even learn basic lessons from my mother. I learned things from other kids, like Joann and Janice who were teenagers I hung out with. They were the ones who taught me the life skills that I would need to know. If it weren't for them, I wouldn't have learned some basic lessons that every child should learn from their mother.

I don't know if I wasn't taught because my mother didn't know how to teach or if she thought the older children would teach me. My siblings taught me some things but when it came to hygiene and how a person should treat others, I didn't learn those skills from them or my mother.

As a child, I wanted to be liked so I searched for things I could do to make others happy. I never felt loved as a child, nor as a teenager; not even as an adult. I had people cross my path who I think God must have put in my life for a reason, but when you are little you don't grasp that, as least I didn't. I will mention some of the people who made a difference in my childhood days only because they helped mold me into what I am today.

There was a missionary family named the Allen's that attended the church where I found refuge. Mrs. Allen taught that I need to wash my hands before I cook. As early as the age of five, I started cooking. I know you are thinking "no way," but I learned out of survival. So then my mother expected me to cook. She did have to read the directions to me. I have cooked Shake-n-Bake until I could scream. But, it was food.

I told Mrs. Allen that I cooked and she didn't really believe me until I told her what I made and how I did it. Then one day she invited my brother Larry and me to come for dinner after church and she asked Larry if I cooked at home. Larry told her that, yes, it was true that I did in fact cook. So, every Sunday I would go to Mrs. Allen's house after church, and she would let me help her in the kitchen. She taught me new recipes and me how important it was to wash my hands and keep everything clean. If she ever would have gone to my house, she probably would have fainted. Not only did my mother not want to cook anymore, but she didn't want to clean house either. I think she had kids just to do that for her. I tried to do my best but I couldn't do it all myself. Tina, my oldest sister, was always gone and my middle sister Linda was always sick. For some reason, when it was time to cook or clean up, Linda would get sick and I was left to do it all. To this day I hate to do dishes, but I do love to cook because food makes people happy. When people are happy, it makes me happy.

Mrs. Allen taught me that I need to thank God for whatever is happening in my life. This family was in my life for a few years, then they had to pack up and go to Hong Kong. I was happy when I was with them. I pretended I was part of their family. They loved each other and I saw that. Sometimes when you see what other people have, you want it for yourself and, yes, I wanted their life. I wanted to eat at the kitchen table and say grace. I wanted plenty of food and to not go to bed hungry. I remember one time that I was so hungry when I was watching the Wizard of Oz that I took salt from a shaker and put it on my hand and sucked it. Did it fill me up and make my stomach not growl? No, of course not. But at the time, I was trying anything to get that awful feeling in the pit of my stomach to go away.

Janice and Joann were the young adults I would hang out with every chance I got. They didn't treat me any differently because I was poor. I think they liked the fact that they were helping me. They asked me questions that made me think. For example, "Do you really need to take a bath every day?" They taught me that if you can't take a bath every day, then you need to at least wash your face and your feet before you go to bed. One night when my mother let me stay at Joann's house, Joann laid a sheet on the couch and asked if I had brushed my teeth and washed my face and feet. I told her yes to brushing my teeth and washing my face. "Why didn't you wash your feet?" Joann asked. I told her, "Because I didn't want to make your white wash cloth turn black." Joann replied, "Are they that dirty?" I could only nod my head yes. Joann then said, "I think you need a bubble bath." I told her I had never had a bubble bath. She smiled at me and told me she would run the water and look for something for me to wear because I hadn't brought anything to sleep in. So that night, I felt like a princess. I had someone draw my bath water. I had someone who was getting me some clothes. It was the most wonderful bath I had ever taken. The water was so warm that I thought it felt like silk. It must have been the bubble bath. When I got out, I smelled like lavender. It was a smell I wasn't accustomed to. I thought to myself how one day I want to have a house with a nice bathtub and different kinds of bubble bath. I laugh now at the simple things I learned from them, but as a child I was amazed.

The one thing about going to Joann's and Janice's house that made a difference for me is, once again, I saw what a family is supposed to be like. Their mother and father provided the things that the children needed. Their parents told the children they loved them and they showed it even more by their actions. Being poor might not have been so bad had I thought I was loved.

CHAPTER 2

Abused as a Child

If being poor wasn't bad enough, I had one more thing that would change me as a child. I was being sexually abused by my mother's boyfriend.

My earliest memories begin with my kindergarten years. I was sick one day and had stayed home from school. My mother's boyfriend came over to see her. Seeing that I was sick, Raymond sent my mother to the corner store to buy some 7-Up. He agreed to watch me until she returned. That was the beginning of years of sexual abuse by him. The abuse did not occur every day, but he took every opportunity he had. Raymond kept me afraid by telling me that if I told anyone about his abuse of me, he would kill my mother in front of me. At the age of five, I loved my mother. So at an early age, I learned to keep secrets.

The abuse would last until I was 15 and would take place every chance that Raymond had. That is why I liked sleeping with Linda and Tina and felt safe with them. That is why I went to church every time I could with my mother's permission. That is why I went to the Allen's. I wish I could have trusted someone to let them know what was going on, but I was threatened that if I told anyone I would be killed or he would kill my mother. No matter how I felt about my mother, I didn't want something to happen to her.

I still remember thinking about what Mrs. Allen told me. I needed to thank God for everything. *But how can you thank God for being sexually abused?* I thought I must be doing something wrong and that God was punishing me. I tried to be a good girl and stay in my mother's good graces. But it didn't matter. I was abused by him no matter how I prayed.

Not only did Raymond sexually abuse me, but he hit me. And the worse thing–if there could be a worse thing– was that he brushed my teeth with Comet.

One day Raymond came in and noticed that Linda's and my teeth weren't white like they should be. We didn't have toothpaste all the time due to the fact that you couldn't buy that with food stamps. So on this day, Raymond told us that he would show us how to brush our teeth. Linda did what she was told, but not me. I was being very stubborn. I would not open my mouth for him to brush my teeth with something that I knew you clean the toilet with. So he grabbed my hair and pulled it hard. I was not going to give in to this monster. Raymond yelled for my mother who came in the bathroom with us, and she told me to open my mouth. I shook my head no. Instead of her speaking up for me like I thought she was going to do, she smacked me in the face. I really did see stars. I was told to open my mouth and do what Raymond told me to do. When I opened my mouth, he brushed my teeth with the Comet. I threw up all over him and me. But that didn't get me anywhere, because then I got sent to my bed without any supper. At that moment, I knew I was on my own for survival. I knew that there was no way that my mother would protect me. Still in the back of my mind I questioned God...*Why?*

From that day on, I stayed away from home as much as I could. I would hunt for glass coke bottles that could be turned in for money, so I could buy things that I needed like toothpaste. I would also go to the Laundromat and take a wire coat hanger to swipe under the washers to see if there were coins. That was a great way to get money, but I had to do it when the owner was not around. I babysat and cleaned houses. I would do anything to make money and to stay out of the house. I would beg my Aunt Delores to take me with her when she came over. Sometimes it worked and sometimes it didn't, but I had to try to go somewhere. Anywhere was safer than the house where I lived.

One summer, I went to camp for a week with Linda. She didn't like it as much as I did. We had a bed of our own and we got three meals a day and even snacks. At night we would have worship and then we sang around the campfire. The night before we had to leave camp, I accepted Jesus in my heart. I got baptized in a creek. When it was time for us to pack up and get ready to board the bus, I started crying. My counselor asked:

"Darlene, what is the matter?"

"I don't want to go home, I want to stay here."

"I am sorry, but you have to go home."

My counselor gave me a hug and helped me get my things together. All the way home I talked to Jesus.

Jesus you know what my home life is like. Can you please help me?

When I got home I didn't share the news with my mother that I had gotten baptized; I didn't know how she would react. Every chance I got after that, I went to church. Portland Christian Church was my refuge.

At home I was being abused, there was never enough food, and each change of season, I was too cold or too hot. Since I got baptized, I talked to Jesus about every day, sometimes three and four times a day. Sometimes I questioned God. *You are a big God. How come you can't take care of me?*

I was eight when I got baptized there at camp. Linda didn't say anything either, for which I was relieved. I also thought if I got baptized, the abuse would stop. I thought God would protect me when I became one of his children. But that didn't happen...the abuse continued.

In 1975 (I was 12), the song *Operator* came out and I said to God: *You know that you and I could have written that song!* I am sure God has a sense of humor and was shaking His head.

I never missed school where I was safe and got two meals a day. I didn't have to worry about anyone bothering me there. I hated the weekends and holidays. Sometimes it seemed like there wasn't enough food to go around. It seemed like we were always wearing old clothes. In the summer, we often didn't wear shoes. One time when one of our uncles died, we had to share boots to go to the funeral. So on the visitation night, Linda wore the boots then I wore them on funeral day. That was sad because I got made fun of by one of my cousins.

Some cousins thought they were better than us. That might be true. But I think if you act ugly then you are ugly. I heard a teacher once say, "If you can't say something nice, then don't say anything at all." I guess their teachers didn't teach them that lesson.

Most children love snow days and I did, too, especially if I had a test that day. But one winter we were living at 22nd and Bank streets, and the house wasn't all that great. It snowed a lot and we were off school. I didn't like this at all. One reason is because Raymond could come by at any time. Another is because the house was so cold. My mother closed off all the rooms in the back, and we all gathered in the living room. There were blankets and pallets everywhere. It was like we were all camping out.

Just like before, there wasn't enough food. My mother's food stamps were gone and she had us all at home to feed. My mother told me to go down to the corner store and ask the owner if we could have some credit. Here I was at age 14, and I was going to ask someone to give us credit until the first of the month. So Tina went with me, and it was cold walking the three blocks we had to walk to the corner store.

The owner knew who we were, which helped a lot. Before I went in, I prayed that I would say the right words so the owner would help us out. I didn't want to go back home empty handed. My mother would not be happy with us if we didn't come back with something.

I went back to the meat counter where the owner was working and, even though I was nervous, I asked, "Sir, do you have a minute?" He turned around and replied, "Do butterflies have wings?" I said, "Yes, they do." He smiled and said, "What can I do for you?" So I began:

> "My mother was wondering if you could give us some food and she will pay you back on the first of the month."

His eyes got sad and I thought the man was going to cry.

> "How many are in your family?"

> "There are four children and my mother at home right now."

He asked about my father, and I told him I didn't have a father.

"Well you are in luck! We are having a sale. If you buy three things you get one free."

"So are you saying we can pay later?"

"Yes, and I will help you pick out the food to get the best deal."

This man had a heart of gold. Did you know that if you bought three cans of pork-n-beans you got a pack of hot dogs free? We also bought three cans of pinto beans and got ten pounds of potatoes. We left there with enough food for a week for twenty dollars!

Yes, I know what you are thinking and I believe it too. The owner of the store felt sorry for my family. I think he must have been a Christian man because he said he would pray for our family.

I didn't leave that store feeling sad. I left there happy that I had food that I could cook and eat. I left there thinking that God helped us that day. I left there thinking that my mother would be so proud of me.

CHAPTER 3

Raped as a Teen

It was not a normal day. After this day my world would forever be changed.

My mother and aunt had to go to the hospital because their mother was going to have an operation. My mother left us home alone. It was me at the age of 15, my niece Debbie who was three, and my brother Larry who was in the back room sleeping. My cousin Mindy was also there that day. She was in the dining room watching TV.

My mother told me when she left that I was in charge and that I needed to feed Debbie and Mindy. I also needed to clean the house before she got home, but she didn't know what time that would be. I thought to myself that I would rather go to school. I couldn't go that day because someone had to watch Debbie. Tina, Debbie's mother, had gotten married and she didn't want to take her baby with her, so my mother agreed to take care of Debbie. I thought Tina should have taken her baby because if she knew what was happening to me, she wouldn't want it to happen to her daughter.

I went back to sleep after my mother gave me the directions. I was still thinking I would rather be at school because I was hungry. I knew that I would get two meals at school. It seemed to me like a few minutes after I went to sleep when I was awakened by a hand over my mouth. I opened my eyes and saw my mother's boyfriend there. He told me not to scream or he would kill Debbie and whoever was in the house. Debbie was sleeping right next to me in the bed. I didn't want her to be scared, so I didn't make a noise. Let me say, I didn't make a noise on the outside of my body but I was screaming on the inside. I could not scream because as I was lying there and being raped, Debbie opened her eyes. Raymond told her everything was ok, and to go back to sleep. He also said that if I didn't lie still, he would do the exact same thing to Debbie. So I did what I could to save her.

I knew what he was doing to my body was wrong, and I also knew that if I made it out of this, I would not return to this house. I had to go someplace in my mind to get through what he was doing to me. So, I imagined I was cooking with Mrs. Allen. I was also praying to God for this all to be over. What seemed like forever did end. After Raymond was done, he removed his hand and told me if I ever told, he would kill me. At that moment, I didn't care. I did say something to him. I said in a whisper, "Go to hell," and got hit in the stomach for it. But Raymond was going to have the last word:

"Next time, I won't be so easy with you."

When he left, I was relieved and I thanked God for getting me through the madness. I laid there until I heard Raymond's van pull away. Then I turned to Debbie and saw that she was asleep. I got up and went to the bathroom where I saw blood and cleaned myself up. As I came out of the bathroom, I noticed that Mindy was still sitting at the table and Larry was still asleep. I wanted to scream, but was too overwhelmed with thoughts of what to do.

The rest of the day, I was in a trance like I was doing things but I really didn't know how I did them. I wanted to cry, but was too scared that someone would notice. So, I turned on the radio and sang to it. Music was also an escape for me. I loved country music and just listening to Barbara Mandrell and the Oak Ridge Boys made me a little bit happy.

When my mother and Aunt Mildred came back, they were laughing and having a great time. They also had empty White Castle bags that they had stopped and bought. Did they bring home White Castle for their children? No. They were out celebrating while a monster was raping me. They didn't even think of their children. I didn't want anything to eat, but I remembered how Debbie liked French fries.

My mother asked me if I got everything done, and I told her yes. I asked my mother how my grandmother was doing. She said my grandmother was fine and that she would have to go up there tomorrow to sit all day, so I would be left home to babysit Debbie again. With that being said, I asked my mother if I could please go to the library to get a few books. Her reply was, "Yes, but make sure you come right back because I want to take a nap."

I got my purse and headed for the door. Before I got to the door, I turned to my mother and wanted to say something, but I just couldn't. When I shut the door I knew I would not go back home; it wasn't a home. It was a place where I hated to be.

For the next few hours, I ran the streets. I did go to the library, because I didn't want to lie to my mother. Then after going there, I went to the In-Out Dairy Mart where I bought a Big Red. The store owner wanted to know why I wasn't in school. I told him that my grandmother had an operation and I was taking care of my niece. He told me I was a good girl and that one day I would make a good mother. I thanked him and left.

I ended up at my old elementary school. It had a staircase where I could hide. I just sat up there and was thinking about what happened that day and what I was going to do. There was no way I could go back home, especially knowing that tomorrow would be the same as today.

This was my safe place. I would come to my old school when I didn't have any other place to go.

Sometimes, like that day, if I had the money I would stop by the store and get a bag of Grippo's and a Big Red. That day I didn't think I could eat potato chips. I was sick inside and just thinking about food made me feel as though I would throw up.

As I sat there, I also thought about all the times I came here. One time was after Raymond came over and touched me in my panties area and was reminding me not to tell anyone. Paul walked in the door and I was so happy. Raymond told my brother Paul that my mother had gone across the street to the beer joint to get a Pepsi. Paul just nodded okay. Raymond told Paul and me to tell our mother he would be back later. I was never so happy that Paul came in and Raymond left. When Raymond left, Paul looked at me and asked me if I was okay. I said yes. Oh, how I wished I could have told Paul the truth, but the threats were playing in my head.

I told Paul I was going to see if Sheila was home. However, I knew where I was really going, so I started walking. On the way, I found a cushion in someone's garbage. I looked around to see if anyone was watching me while I got that cushion out of the garbage. I knew they had thrown it away, but I didn't want to get in trouble either. So on that day when I climbed those steps, I put that cushion on the concrete and sat down. I got a book out of my purse and started reading, because the books I read would take me anywhere. They took me to faraway lands. I was not scared when I read my books.

As I looked down at my hands, now they were empty. My Big Red was barely touched and today I didn't stop to get the cushion from the side of the house. I just wanted to get out of my house. I am not sure how long I sat there, but I knew it was getting late.

Well, I am afraid of the dark, so when it got real dark I had to decide what to do next. I knew that there was a firehouse right around the corner, so I walked there. What I was going to do when I got there, I didn't know, but I knew that I would be safe there. So, I rang the doorbell and the captain came to the door.

He smiled and asked me if there was a problem. I told him that I needed to talk to someone. He said that I could tell him. For some reason, I knew I could. So I told him I was being abused by someone and I didn't want to go home. He told me that he could call someone and that they would come and talk to me. I told him I would have to think about it. So, he led me to an open living room. There were other firemen in there and they looked at the captain and left. I told him that they didn't have to leave. He told me that it was okay; they are nice men and if I needed help, I could talk to anyone of them. He was trying so hard to get me to agree to call someone.

I told him "thanks but no thanks" because I needed to go. He in no way wanted me to leave. As I was leaving, I heard him on the phone calling for the police. I just kept on walking. I thought to myself that the police were just going to make it worse.

As I got down the street, I heard sirens but I also heard a horn honking. It was a car, and it had my mother in it. She got out and started towards me, fussing that I should have been home hours ago. Well, with all my strength, I screamed at the top of my lungs that I wasn't going back home because I was raped today.

Out of the corner of my eye, I saw the captain talking to a policeman and then I turned to look at my mother. My mother just looked at me and said, "By whom?" I told her, "By your boyfriend." Right there in the middle of Portland Street, my mother fainted.

Chaos broke loose and I felt a hand on my shoulder. It was the captain. He said:

"I didn't get your name."

"It is Darlene."

"Well, I am proud of you for telling. Please just know that God loves you."

The look on my face was probably one of relief because he said, "I am glad you believe like I do."

I wish I could have gotten his name before I was rushed off to the house of my mother's friend, Carla. There my mother was just crying, and there was a policeman, Officer Miller, telling my mother she had no choice but to take me to the hospital. My mother's friend Carla told her she would take me. I looked at my mother and asked her if she was going with me. She said no, that she couldn't handle it. I don't know what got into me, but that was the first time that I back talked my mother. I said to her, "Well, do you think *I* can handle it?"

Officer Miller did offer my mother an opportunity to ride with me in the police car, but she said no. She asked the policeman if she could have Carla bring me instead of me riding in the police car. They agreed, but they said they would follow the car.

So, off I went to the hospital with Carla. She was really nice and tried to make small talk, but I wasn't interested. I just felt so alone. The rape was bad, but what I was feeling was betrayal by the person who gave birth to me.

When Carla and I got to the hospital, Officer Miller talked to the nurse then I was led to a room. I didn't have to wait in the waiting room. I was asked if I wanted Carla with me and I said no. The nurse said that they would have to examine me and collect evidence. I did what I was told about taking my clothes off and putting on the gown. I wanted to be anywhere but there. Well, not really...I didn't want to go home. I didn't want to see my mother.

The nurse let me hold her hand while a doctor examined me and collected whatever they needed. I didn't talk, but I cried. Tears were streaming down my face. The nurse was so kind to me that she wiped my face and told me that it would be over soon. The doctor was a man. I knew there were women doctors, but with my luck there was no woman doctor on call that night. The doctor told me everything he was doing and was so kind with his words. However, at that moment I wanted nothing more than this nightmare to be over. After the examination, the doctor told me that I would be given a pill to take tonight and another one to be taken in the morning. This was a precaution in case I had conceived a baby during the rape. I felt like I had no say in the matter at all. I was then told that I could put some clothes on. I looked at the nurse and asked, "What clothes?" She gave me a smile and said she would find me something.

"Will you be ok if I leave for a moment?" she asked, and I told her yes. While she was gone, a woman from the rape crisis center came in. She told me her name was Pam and that she would be there for me. She wanted to know if there was anything I needed. I said, "Yes...a new life." When I told Pam that the nurse was looking for some clothes for me, she said, "Well you are in luck. I have clothes in my car. I will go and get you some."

Pam asked me what size I wore, left like a flash, and returned just as fast. I went into the restroom and changed out of the gown. The reflection I saw in the mirror was a scared girl. I was looking at me and I didn't understand what I had done so wrong to get this treatment.

When I came out, the nurse was there along with Pam from the rape crisis center, plus Officer Miller. I could tell that they were uncomfortable, too, but they all had a job to do. *If only I would have told someone sooner; I wouldn't be in this mess now.*

Officer Miller said that he wanted to take me down to the police station for a statement. Pam, who was too bubbly for me at the present time, said that she would go, too. I tried so hard not to be rude to her, but I told her that I didn't need her to go with me. She reached into her pocket and pulled out a business card and told me that I could call anytime to talk to someone. I thanked her and she left. Officer Miller looked at me and asked if I was ready. I wasn't, but I didn't think I had a choice.

Carla was outside in the waiting room and she jumped up as soon as she saw us come out. Officer Miller informed Carla that they will take me down to the police station for me to give a statement. Carla asked him if I could ride with her. He said we could do whatever I wanted to do. I said it didn't matter to me. But as we were walking to the parking lot, I chose to get in the police car. I felt safer there. He was a man with authority and he had a gun. He would protect me.

It is rather odd that everyone was treating me like I was going to break, or as if they just didn't know if I was going to freak out. Officer Miller had to call my mother and get permission to take the statement and Carla had to sign her name, too, because I was a minor.

The questions that were asked were hard. I had to go over everything again, but Officer Miller was so nice. I looked up at him one time and said, "Can I ask you a question?" He said yes, and so I asked him if he had any kids. His answer was yes. I then asked, "If your daughter was raped, would you still love your daughter?" It took him a moment to respond, because I think he was taken aback with what I had just asked him.

"Darlene, in no way was this was your fault. I think in time you will realize that, and yes, I would love my daughter with all my heart."

A single tear went down the side of my face.

After about an hour, we were through with the statement and I was free to go. Officer Miller told Carla that some detectives would be in touch with my mom in a day or two. He shook my hand and told me that he was proud of me. I just said, "Thanks."

As we were leaving, Carla asked if I wanted to get something to eat. "No" was my reply, and so we drove toward home. I got a little bit nervous because I thought we were going back to my house. I think Carla could sense it and told me that she was taking me back to her house. I relaxed then.

As we walked into Carla's house, there were people from her family but my brothers and sisters were also there. Everyone was quiet. It was like someone had died. I went into the living room and found my mother asleep on the couch. *How could she sleep at time like this?* I soon found out that someone had called her doctor who called in some medicine for her. The thought going through my head was that the person who called my mother's doctor was not very nice. *My mother should be going through the same hell I am going through!* I figured that by the time my mother woke up, this would be over with. Not. But I think that was what my mother was thinking.

They tried to wake my mother up when I arrived, but it didn't work. I felt sad for Carla's family because all of my family was going to stay there and we were invading their house. Carla asked me if there was anything that she could do for me. I asked her if I could take a shower. She said yes and went to get me some towels. When Carla came back, she brought me clothes, too. I thanked her for all the things she was doing for me and my family. She told me that is what friends are for.

I showered until I couldn't stand the hot water any more. I then went out and found everyone in beds, on the floor, and everywhere. Carla had made a pallet for me on the floor. I must had fear in my eyes because she asked if I wanted to sleep with her. I said yes, and went and got in her bed. She had a round, red velvet bed. It was neat. I would have liked to have slept there on a normal day. Carla told me if I wanted to sleep late the next day, I could, and told me again that she was proud of me. She also let me know I could stay at her house for as long as I wanted. I just told her thanks again and tried so hard not to cry. But she could see that I had tears in my eyes.

Sleep did come, but it was not a good sleep. I was restless. I was going over and over everything that happened that day.

In the morning, I woke up and found the house still quiet and walked to the kitchen. I noticed all the kids were gone. It was a school day. So, life does go on. Life didn't stop because I got raped. It still went on. I thought they were leaving me home because they still needed a babysitter for Debbie, but that had changed, too. Debbie went to my Aunt Gwen's house and Mindy went along to watch her. In the kitchen, Carla was sitting at the table and drinking coffee.

"Can I have a cup, too?"

"Sure, but are you too young to drink coffee?"

My reply to her was that I have been drinking coffee all my life. Then I went on to tell her that I liked to have milk and sugar in mine.

I wanted to say so much to Carla, but I really didn't know how much I could say. I really didn't trust people anymore. The people that were supposed to protect me had failed me. I decided just to make small talk. I did ask how long my mother would be sleeping.

"I really don't know. I think we will give her a few more hours, then try to get her up and have her take a shower. I just guess she doesn't know how to deal with it."

My only reply was, "Like I do?" I sat there thinking about how I was going to get through the day. When there was a knock at the door, I went to answer it because Carla only had a robe on.

I looked out the window and saw that it was Aunt Delores, so I opened the door. My aunt just hugged me and I knew that there was one person that I could count on. She started talking and asking questions. I just shook my head and said, "You need to slow down." She laughed and said, "I know." Then she wanted to know where my mother was.

I told her, "She's still sleeping on the couch. She's been there since we got home from me telling her what happened." So, Aunt Delores went into the living room and tried to wake mother up with no luck.

"Well Darlene, what do you want to do since your mother is in wonderland?"

"Honestly, I want to get out of here. Do you think I can go home with you? I promise that I will be good and I will help you clean and I will cook for you."

"Yes, you can come and you don't have to cook or clean. There are a few things I need to do this morning, but you can ride with me."

Carla came in the room, and Aunt Delores told her that I was going home with her. Carla said that would be a good thing but the detectives' might come to see me. My Aunt Delores said if they did, just call her and she would bring me back.

In a shaky voice I said, "I don't have any clothes here." "No problem. We can buy you some," Aunt Delores told me. I was very thankful that I wouldn't have to go to my house right now.

I did ask my aunt, "What about mother? Will she be mad that I left?" Aunt Delores said she didn't care at the moment, and Carla said she would explain that I, too, needed a break. Still, I didn't want my mother to be mad at me and I thought that was dumb since she had not been there for me. As we were driving away, Aunt Delores said that I could stay with her as long as I wanted and that she would bring me back every day for school. I just said, "Thank you." We ran a lot of errands and then went across the K & I bridge to Indiana. That is where Aunt Delores and Uncle Elmer lived.

As we walked in, Uncle Elmer was lying on the couch. He is so funny. When he lies like that and eats and smokes, he doesn't even get choked. My Uncle Elmer is a man of very few words. I have never heard him talk in sentences. It was always in short answers. I said "Hi" to him and I sat down on the other couch. He said, "Hi," and asked my aunt if she got what I needed. Aunt Delores told him, yes, we went shopping and that I would be with them for a while. My uncle said, "Good."

The rest of the day, I was just sitting around and watching TV. I also helped with dinner and cleaned up afterwards. I was very happy that I was in a safe place. I was happy that Aunt Delores and Uncle Elmer didn't ask me any questions. They just let me be. At night Aunt Delores brought me sheets so I could sleep on the couch. They did have another bedroom, however it was full of my uncle's tools and my aunt's sewing stuff. But I didn't care. I was happy to sleep on the couch. I was here with them and I was safe. I didn't have to worry about going to sleep.

> *God, are you listening? I know my mother is probably real mad at me. Is there some way you can get her to see that what he did was wrong? And God, thanks for sending my aunt to get me. Amen.*

The next morning, Aunt Delores and Uncle Elmer went to work, and I was left to myself. I loved it. Aunt Delores told me to make myself at home. She told me that my uncle would be in and out to check on me, and I thought that was nice. She had to work until 3:30. I watched a little TV, then went and took a long bath. It was so nice to be by myself and to not be afraid. I then washed clothes for my Aunt Delores. I knew I had to go back home soon and the thought just scared me. I knew I would have to face life soon. I hadn't heard from my mother yet. *She must be really mad at me and her boyfriend.* I tried very hard to not think of things because I needed to take this time that I had for myself.

Well, my mother called two days after I went to stay with Aunt Delores. She only talked with my aunt and told her I needed to be back at the house around noon. It was a Saturday and my Aunt Delores said she would have me there on time. My Aunt Delores told me, "You know you can come back." I just nodded my head.

On the way home, I was very quiet. I wanted to return to my aunt's house after I finished in Louisville. Officer Miller and a Detective Lane met us at my house and I just stood outside on the sidewalk. Detective Lane asked me how I was doing. I told him I was okay. He then asked me, "Can you please go inside with us and tell us where all this took place?"

I was so short with Officer Miller and I had no right to be. I told him that there were already people there who knew. I also explained how they said someone came the night I went to the hospital and took the sheets off the bed. I asked him who would be in the room with us. He said I could have anyone I wanted. I told Officer Miller that I just wanted him and Detective Lane, no one else. So, the three of us went into the house and back to the bedroom. The only thing that was different, in fact, was the removal of the sheets from the bed. Nobody had done the dishes, nobody picked up the trash, nothing. It appeared to me as if nobody had been living in the house.

Officer Miller cleared his throat and said, "Darlene are you ready to start telling us what happened?" I wasn't ready, but I had no choice but to tell these men what happened again. They asked very few questions and then said that they had enough information. I couldn't get out of the house quick enough.

My mother was talking to Aunt Delores and I could tell she was not happy. I went over to mother hoping for a hug, but it didn't come. She did say that I could go back to my aunt's but only until she moved from this house. Carla was moving and my mother talked to the owner of that house who agreed to let my mother rent the house. I thought that would be great since I didn't want to go back to the house where I'd been raped.

My mother didn't ask how I was doing or hug me, or anything. It was like she wasn't even there. She did say that I had to go back to school and that I needed to think about going to counseling. I just looked at her and said okay.

31

My days ran one into another. It took a few months before I had to go to court, which I really didn't want to do. My mother treated me differently! I just stayed in my room as much as I could. I did go to the rape crisis center but that was a joke. Pam told Linda, who went with me, that the chances of me turning gay were great. Well, they didn't know what they were talking about at that center, so I told my mother that I didn't need to go back.

Then I had to meet with a prosecutor named Mr. White. That was a day I didn't like. He asked in front of my mother if the rape was the first time that her boyfriend touched me. Well, I show my feelings on my face even when I don't want to. So I wouldn't talk. Mr. White then asked my mother to leave the room. She was not happy because she couldn't hear what I had to say. The look that she gave me before she left the room was not one of love. It was of hate.

Mr. White was nice and I answered his questions. It was like I didn't care anymore whether my mother was happy with me. *What more could I lose? There has to be a reason why things happen.*

Mr. White asked again if the rape was the first time and I said yes, however he had been doing other things to me for years. After a brief second, the prosecutor asked, "How many?" I looked him in the eyes and told him it had been going on for at least ten years. Mr. White asked me to start from the beginning. So I did. We took a break when I had to go to the restroom. Mr. White was even nice enough to buy me dinner. It was just pizza that someone had brought in. I didn't eat very much, but it was nice that he thought of my well-being. Not even my own mother was thinking of that. Overall, it took 3 to 4 hours for Mr. White to question me. I know he had other people to talk to, but today was my day to be listened to, and I spilled all I had in me. On that day, I decided I would not be silent. *If someone asks me something from now on, I will tell them. I will not live in fear.*

When I walked out of there, the prosecutor told my mother that with new evidence, her boyfriend would be spending a lot of time in jail.

After we left the courthouse, we went back to the house my mother had moved into while I was over at my aunt's house. My mother was very quiet. It scared me. I followed her into the house and noticed it looked nice. It was clean. My mother said that my room was upstairs. So I went upstairs and there was a bed and one dresser, nothing else. However, I loved it because I now had a room to myself.

I went downstairs and my mother was in the kitchen sitting at the kitchen table drinking coffee and smoking a cigarette. I said, "Thanks, mother, for the room. I like it." "Good" was all she said. My mother treated me differently and it seemed like she was mad all the time.

The next morning, I was taking a bath and shaving my legs when my mother opened the door to the bathroom without knocking. It scared me so that I jumped and cut my leg shaving. Blood started going everywhere. I grabbed a wash cloth and applied it to my leg. My mother sat down on the toilet. She had a cigarette in her hand.

"Is there anything wrong, mother?"

"Darlene, there is no easy way to tell you this, so I am going to just come right out and tell you and then I will answer any questions you have. Your Uncle Elmer is not your uncle. He is your father."

The air went out of my lungs. *Well, I didn't expect that.* I asked my mother:

"Could you please tell me how that is possible?"

"When I was dating your father, we lived together for about seven years. Then we broke up after your baby brother David passed away. Then Aunt Delores and your father started dating and soon got married. Your father's name is even on your birth certificate. However, when you started school, I thought it was best that all my children have the same name so I went and changed your and Linda's last names. You and Linda were the only ones who had your father's last name."

"Well, I guess that explains why when we were little you would let Aunt Delores come and take me and Linda over to their house. That would explain why they bought us clothes. That explains why my father would come and get Terry and Larry to help him some times. That would explain why you would send us to the junk yard where our Uncle Elmer worked to get money from him because we needed food. My only question I have for you is, 'Why didn't someone tell me sooner? Why did you have to wait until I was raped to tell me that I do have a father?'"

"I wanted it that way. There is no way I was going to let them take my children. I needed all my children to live with me."

"But mother, I have asked you over and over who my father was and you would just tell me to shut up or that it was none of my business!"

"Well, you left me no choice. You had Raymond arrested, and now we have to go to court. I'm afraid it might come out in the trial. I wanted you to hear it from me."

"Mother, I didn't have Raymond arrested. He raped me."

My mother didn't say another word. She got up and walked out.

I sat in the tub until the water turned ice cold. When I got out, I wasn't cold. I think I was numb. *My mother is blaming me for the rape.*

All I could think of is how I needed to get out of there and take a walk. I walked to the church by my house. I went in and I asked the lady there if I could go pray. She asked me if I was okay, and I told her yes. I sat on the first pew and prayed:

> *God, I hope you are listening to me. I don't really know what to do now. Please tell me what to do. Amen.*

I started going to that church and it helped while I was going through the trial. I wished Mrs. Allen was back from Hong Kong so I could go and talk to her. Then I remembered one of the Bible verses she told me: "I can do all this through him who gives me strength" (Phil. 4:13 NIV).

Church was my answer. I went there to escape the looks my mother was giving me. I went there to pray to God. I went there for the music. I went there for strangers to love on me. I needed and wanted to be loved.

Church became my home away from home. One day I asked my mother if I could go to church and she said, "I don't care what you do anymore." "Mother, will you ever love me again?" I asked with tears in my eyes. My mother did not answer the question. From that day on, I didn't ask if I could go to church anymore.

My mother went to court with me the day of the trial and I was happy because I honestly thought she wouldn't. When I got to the courtroom, the lawyer for my case was different. I guess it was because I couldn't afford one and this one was mine now. I saw that they had the fire captain there. I didn't want to look at Raymond, so I just kept my head down.

I took the stand. I had to tell them what happened again. I was thinking this was worse than the rape...telling all these people what happened to me.

The lawyers and judge talked and it so happened that they made a plea deal. Raymond got six months in jail that he would serve on the weekends since he had a family at home, and he got five years' probation. He wasn't allowed to come around me. *That's it? He sexually abused me for ten years and raped me and that's all he gets?!*

My mother told me to get up, and I was walking but I don't really know how. When we went out of the courtroom, I saw the Captain from the firehouse in the hall and I walked over to him and I told him I was sorry that they dragged him into it. The Captain extended his hand to shake my hand.

"I am Captain Ernie. Darlene, you have no reason to be sorry. I wish you the best."

My mother was yelling for me to come back over to where she and Aunt Delores were standing.

Aunt Delores drove us home and I asked if I could go over to my aunt's house. My mother said no. I didn't say anything else. I just went to my room and cried.

I think I was crying because the trial was over. I was crying because I could feel that my mother was mad at me. I was crying because I had found out I had a father, but couldn't go see him.

In a few days, I started to feel a little better about myself even though my mother wasn't really talking to me. I still went to church every chance I got and was trying to understand my feelings and trying to go to school and still act like there was nothing was going on in my life. I didn't tell anyone at school the hell I was going through at home.

One morning I couldn't believe it when my mother told me that she and Debbie would be going to church with me on Sunday. I was so excited! We continued going to church every Sunday. I made a decision that I needed to get baptized for the right reason, not because I thought the abuse would stop. I still didn't tell my mother how I had gotten baptized in the creek at camp. I didn't want to spoil the feeling that this could be the beginning of healing for the both of us. My mother and I got baptized on the same day. I was happy my mother was doing something this big with me. Maybe this is what we needed.

After being baptized, I sat down beside my mother. I had a smile on my face. I heard someone come in and then that someone sat behind us in a pew. The hairs on the back of my neck stood up. When I turned and saw who it was, my smile faded as I looked into Raymond's face. The fear was too great and I got up and I walked out. My mother came out after me and wanted to know what was the matter. Well, I told her that I was not sitting by him and that he was not even supposed to be around me. She was mad as hell at me and told me that the trial was over and it was time for us to move on. She went back into the church and got Raymond.

As I was standing there, I was wondering what I was going to do. I then remembered that my father and Aunt Delores had moved to Kentucky and their house was not far from there. So when my mother and Raymond came back out, I told my mother that I was going to my father's house.

"You can't. We are going to take you to lunch, to celebrate."

"You want me to celebrate with him? HAVE YOU LOST YOUR MIND?!!"

You would think I would get used to being smacked in the face, but I didn't. It still threw me off and I just stood there enraged. I looked at my mother and said, "I am going to my father's house. If you try to stop me I will call the police and tell them that you are letting Raymond hang around me. I don't think they, or the judge, will be happy with you, Mother." I turned around and walked to my father's house. While I was walking, it felt good to know that I had a father whose house I could go to.

As I walked, I prayed that somehow things would work out. How was I going to live with my mother who was mad at me all the time? Plus, now Raymond was back and the way he looked at me gave me the feeling I would not be safe at my mother's house.

It was not a far walk at all. I didn't even know if they would be home, but God was smiling on me that day because they were both there. My cousins from Evansville were there visiting, and I told them what had happened at the church. My cousin's wife, Marcie, asked me if I wanted to come and stay with them for a while. I said sure, but I also said that I didn't know if my mother would say it was okay. My father, who says very little, said that he would talk to her if she said no. I told them I needed to go get my clothes and Marcie said she would go with me.

So, Aunt Delores and Marcie went with me to the house to pack. We packed all the clothes that were mine. Some were dirty, so I had to have two bags. Marcie said that was okay because I could wash them when we got to her home. Since there was no one at the house, I left a note for my mother:

> *Mother, I am sorry it has come to this but I need a break from this madness in the life I am living. I will be going home with Marcie and Tim to Evansville and will be staying with them for a little while. Father said if you had any problem with this you could talk to him.*

> *Love, Darlene*

As I looked at the word *love*, I just wondered if my mother loved me back.

As we drove over the bridge later that day, I thought: *Oh, the freedom!* I felt so great! I was going to be free at last.

Sitting between Tim and Marcie in the front seat of their blue Impala felt so good. Their three children, Ben, Luke and Tara, rode in the back seat and even they seemed happy that I was going home with them.

I was thinking...*Indiana here I come!*

CHAPTER 4

Moving Out at the Age of 15

Moving to Evansville was the greatest thing I could have done.

The first weekend was really boring and I thought I had moved to a different country. But one day while the children were at school, my cousin Marcie and her friend Donna took me downtown. While we were waiting to cross the street, a motorcycle slowed down because the light was getting ready to change. I said that I wanted to ride the bike. Well, the driver heard me and told me to come on. So, off I went. I didn't even think about it. There I was on the back of a motorcycle and I didn't even know who the driver was. I couldn't even see his face because he had a helmet on. But, oh, it felt so good to be on the back of a motorcycle. That was my first motorcycle ride. The man drove me around a few blocks and took me right back where he picked me up.

Marcie and Donna were sitting on a bench waiting for me. I walked over to Marcie and she hugged me. She said, "What would your mother say if I called her and told her I couldn't find Darlene?" Then Marcie, pretending to be on the phone with my mother, said, "I am sorry to tell you this, but Darlene decided to lose her brain for a minute and got on the back of a motorcycle with God-knows-who." I just laughed out loud and said, "You must have forgotten who my mother is!" I did promise Marcie that I wouldn't do that again.

After the first week of staying with Tim and Marcie, I just knew I couldn't go back to Louisville. While Tim was at work, I asked Marcie if there was any chance I could live with them. "I know I'm asking a lot of you and Tim, but I just can't go back home and I'm afraid of what would happen if I did." Marcie came over to where I was standing and gave me a hug. "I will talk to Tim and see what he thinks." I told her that they wouldn't even know I was there if they would let me stay.

The next day we went to Central High School to ask some questions about my attending there when school started. We were told it would cost a lot of money because I was not one of their children, nor did they have any papers saying I could live there. So after Marcie and I got home, we talked to Tim about it. I emphasized to them that I didn't want to go home, that I would be good and not cause any problems at all. Marcie cleared her throat and winked at me. I then went on to say that I would do my very best to do what is right. So the next day, Marcie and

Tim made some phone calls and found out that I could live with them but I would have to go in front of a judge to say that no one is forcing me to live with them.

After what I had been through, I wasn't afraid to talk to a judge. I was scared of what my mother was going to think and say. Would she make me come back because she was getting a check because of me? After spending just a small amount of time with Tim and Marcie and their children, I knew I could not go back to my mother's house—even if that meant I would have to run away and live on the streets!

Luckily, I didn't have to live on the streets because the judge granted Tim and Marcie guardianship. He did ask me if I was being forced to live there and I told him no. I then asked him a question.

"I have had a terribly bad year involving rape. My mother has decided to go back to her boyfriend who was the rapist. Is there any way my mother can come up here and take me from them and cause them trouble?"

The judge told me that I was of the age of consent and I could decide where I wanted to live and with whom.

"With the details of your life, there is no way that Tim and Marcie could get in trouble. The trouble will be for your mother if she wants to challenge this ruling, because I will then have no other choice but to charge her with child endangerment."

I felt so much better because I wanted to live in Indiana and I wanted to know that my mother didn't have a legal right to me after what she had put me through.

As I was walking out of the courthouse, I said, "Do you both know what this means?" They both looked at me puzzled. "It means my father is my grandpa, too." Marcie asked, "How is that?"

"Well, you just got guardianship of me. Which makes Aunt Delores my grandma, and since my father is married to your mom, Tim, that makes him my grandpa."

We all three just started laughing. I was happy going to a home that would be mine. I was going to be able to stay and go to school.

My mother was also relieved that I was staying in Indiana. It made her life easier because now she could date Raymond.

The next weekend, we went to my cousin's company picnic and, as we were driving up, I saw about 5 or 6 motorcycles. Marcie looked at me and sternly said, "I don't care who owns those, you will not be riding on them." As it turned out, one of those motorcycles belonged to a young man whose name was Darrel; he worked with Tim. I was on the back of that motorcycle all day long. It was great. When it was time for the picnic to end, Darrel wanted to know if I wanted to go eat with him and his friends. I had to go ask permission, and Darrel told me that he would take me home. Marcie didn't really want me to go, but Tim knew Darrel very well and said that I could. Marcie told me to be good and have fun. I hugged her and told her thanks.

We went to Burger King and, as I was sitting there, I realized this was my first outing with a boy. Well, actually, I was out with a man because Darrel was five years older than me. Darrel was very nice and polite. At no time was he out of line. He said, "I love to hear you talk. You sound country." I was from Louisville and had never lived in the country. But when you come to Indiana from Kentucky, everyone thinks you are from the country.

There were things I had to get used to living in Indiana. One of them was not having to cook or clean the house unless I wanted to. I only had to keep my room clean. I had to go to church, which wasn't that big of a deal because I liked church. The difference was that I was used to going to a Baptist church and now I would be going to a Church of God. The church was little which made it seem like I was someone, because everyone got to know your name. I soon liked this church, too, especially the music.

School was hard only because I was the country girl from Louisville. But I made A's and B's and also made some great friends. Life was a whole lot easier there. I soon got a job at Wendy's and had money. Tim and Marcie said I needed to give God his 10% and maybe more if I wanted to. I then needed to save 15 % and the rest I could do with what I wanted. I tried to give them some money, but they never took it. Sometimes I would pay for a meal if Marcie and I went out. They wanted me to pay for my personal expenses since they had three children. I could understand that, so I paid for whatever I needed and anything else I wanted to do. I am so happy that God put Marcie and Tim and their family in my life.

I am also happy that God put Darrel in my life, because he was a great listener and he was nice to me. I have some really good memories of my times with him.

I was missing home. Can you believe that? One Saturday, Darrel drove me to Louisville on his motorcycle. Two hours on a motorcycle that I wasn't used to was still great. I loved showing him where I lived. My mother seemed happy to see me, but I think it was only in front of Darrel. After we left my mother's house, we went downtown and ate at a Long John Silver's. It was a hot day. While we were eating, a policeman came up to us and asked us if we were driving a motorcycle. Well, that was a stupid question since we had helmets. Darrel said yes and then he told us that the motorcycle had fallen over and hit a car. *Great!*

We went outside and, sure enough, there was the bike over on the ground. The car didn't really look hurt but it did have a scratch on it, so Darrel and the lady exchanged names and phone numbers. I know it was not my fault but when things went bad, I felt that in some way it is my fault.

We left to head back to Evansville after that. It took us longer to get back because we had problems with the motorcycle. It was leaking oil. We stopped at Darrel's house and went in for a minute. His mother and father said that Marcie had already called to see if we had made it back to their house yet. So I called Marcie from there and told her that we were at Darrel's and that we were leaving. Darrel's mother gave me a sweater to wear because it was cold outside now that the sun had gone down. It was also because I had oil all over my arm and top. I didn't want to put the sweater on because, for one, it was white and I don't wear white well, and another reason was my fear that I would get oil on the sweater. She assured me that she didn't need the sweater and that, if it got ruined, it would be okay.

We got in Darrel's car and he drove me home. As we were driving, he told me that in no way was it my fault for the bike falling. It was his, because he should have known that it was a hot day and that he should have put a piece of board under the kickstand. I am glad he said what he did, but I still felt responsible for the accident.

That was the last long trip we took on the motorcycle, but not the only accident I had on that same motorcycle. I did try to drive it with Darrel behind me. I laid the bike down and got a horrible burn on my leg. I will never try to drive a bike again. I just like sitting behind the driver and enjoying the ride.

Darrel came into my life when I needed a man to make me feel good. He listened to everything I said. He gave advice and didn't judge me for my past. I guess you could say that he was my first love, and I will never forget what he gave me.

Central High School was so different than the high school that I had gone to in Louisville. The teens here got to leave for lunch and come back after they were done with their lunch. The school was cleaner. The kids had parents who really cared about their children. It was like there were lots of people always being positive. I realized one day that it wasn't the city, school or even my peers. It was me. It was me changing into a normal teenager who didn't have anything to feel scared about now. It was me learning how to laugh. It was me feeling good about myself.

My last year of high school, Darrel and I stopped being boyfriend and girlfriend. In no way did we break up as friends. My heart will always hold a special place for him because he made a huge difference in my life.

I finished high school with A's and B's. I was so happy to graduate from high school. Out of six children, there were only two of us who graduated.

Even though I was abused for a long time, I still had the feeling that there were good men out there. I didn't want to be afraid of males. When I was little, I was searching for a real mother. Now, I was searching for a real man.

CHAPTER 5

Returning to Louisville

When Darrel and I broke up, I was sad. Tim and Marcie told us that the next weekend we would be going to Louisville for a visit. While we were down there, I had a blind date. He was the brother of my sister-n-law Jamie. We went and watched the movie *Smoky and the Bandit*.

I think it is funny because, after that, we didn't talk for a few months because Clint said I was rude when he took me home. Clint claimed that I asked my mother if Darrel had called. I still don't remember asking her that. Clint was also mad because he had paid for dinner and a movie and didn't even get a kiss from me.

One day out of the blue, I called Clint to see if he was home, but his mother said that he was at work. She took my name and number and told me that she would have Clint call me. Well, I was told that when Clint came home, she did tell him and he asked, "Who is Darlene?" His mother told him, "You know, Terry's sister." Clint did return my call, and then we started writing to each other. Every day I would send Clint a letter in the mail.

We became girlfriend and boyfriend through our letters. Sometimes the letters from him were short, but it didn't matter. I would race off the school bus to see if I had a letter there waiting for me. Most days I did.

I really needed to decide what I was going to do after graduation. I finally decided. On graduation day, I was going back home with Clint and his sister Jamie. I was going to live with Terry and Jamie. I wanted to go back home, but I had mixed emotions.

It was hard to make the decision because I liked living in Evansville. I didn't have a plan of what I was going to do after school. Things were also changing at my cousin's house. Tim went back into the service and Marcie was left to raise their children and me. I started feeling like I was a burden to her because they were having trouble with finances. The family that saved me from staying at my mother's house was changing.

Marcie and Tim did a great job taking care of me but it was time for me to move on, and I knew that. Marcie didn't want me to go and was thinking that I was moving out because of her. I assured her that it was not her and that I would stay in touch and come back to visit.

CHAPTER 6

Getting Married

When I crossed that bridge from Indiana to Kentucky, I was not as happy as I was when I did the opposite two years earlier.

As I was driving back to Louisville with Clint and my sister-in-law Jamie, I didn't have a clue what I would be doing. I knew I would have to find a job, and I knew that I needed to find a church where I would be happy.

I did find a job at Druthers' Restaurant close to the apartment where I was living. I was able to walk from the apartment to work. Walking was my only way of getting around except for when Clint and Jamie were not working. They would drive me if I needed to go somewhere far. Terry worked a lot, so it was hard for him to take me places.

After that, I got a job at Wendy's. I liked it better because I got more hours. I also liked the food there better than the food at Druthers'. However, it was a mile and a half from the apartment, so I got more exercise.

Terry and Jamie were buying a house close to Wendy's. I liked that because I would have a shorter walk. Well, what I didn't know was that God had a different plan for me. That plan was to go to work for an auto parts store as a driver. It was about three to four miles away. I liked to walk, but it would've been hard to get there in the morning. Clint could pick me up on the way home from his job but getting to work was going to be a problem.

As I was trying to decide if I wanted to take the job, Clint came home and said he had found me a car. The car was a 1976 Pacer and the man only wanted $200 dollars for it. I didn't know what a Pacer was, but Clint said it was a good car and that we could go look at it. We did and it looked like a space ship to me. I wrote a check out for it that night. I drove it to Clint's house because he and his father were going to look it over and fix some minor problems. The first thing they fixed was the radio. I like to have music in my life. There were other minor repairs they did, and then I was all set to go driving in my Pacer.

I started working at the auto parts store as a driver. I loved it because I got to drive all over Louisville and I was making good money. I was able to save more and had a feeling that Clint was getting serious about our relationship.

Clint asked me to marry him on Easter. I didn't realize what he was doing, because he gave me a small basket with a ring tied to the side of it. I didn't understand what he was asking. Jamie was laughing at me. She said, "You silly girl. He wants you to marry him." I was so happy. I was happy because Clint wanted me as his wife. However, his father was not happy. My future father-in-law thought I wasn't good enough for his son. Maybe this was just my interpretation. I think it is hard to let your children go.

So we started planning a wedding. It would take place on June 30th. I didn't have much money, so I went to ask my father if he would just pay for the cake. He said he would. Aunt Delores said that she would make my veil and I went searching for a simple dress, which I found at J.C. Penny's for $99 dollars. It was nothing fancy, but it was me. I loved the dress.

Our pastor, Brother Dorsey, asked Clint if he had asked my father for permission to marry me. He said no and then Pastor Dorsey said that he needed to do it. That was very hard for Clint to do, but we went down on a Friday afternoon after he got off work. My father was there as was Aunt Delores. Clint asked him if it was okay to marry me. My father, a man of very few words, said, "Yes, I guess so. I am paying for the cake. There has to be a wedding." I was relieved that it went well.

Nervously I told my father I had one question, too. *Would he walk me down the aisle?* My father didn't go to church, and I just didn't think he would do it. I was wrong.

My father said he would. After we left there, I was happy, very happy.

There was one more stop we needed to make while we were down in Portland. It was my mother's house. At this time in my mother's life, she was married to Jason, so I thought it would be different. It was not. There was still a tone in her voice like I was bothering her. I did the talking and told her and Jason that Clint and I were going to get married. I didn't ask her permission. I was just stating the facts. At no time did she say that she was happy for us. She did say that she would not pay for anything. That was no surprise to me.

As we left my mother's house, I felt a little sad, but not much. I guess I was getting what I deserved since I did leave her home. Clint asked me what her problem was. I told Clint then about the rape and told him I would understand if he didn't want to marry me. He told me that he loved me and still wanted to marry me and spend the rest of our lives together.

I then confided in Clint that I thought that his father didn't like me. He told me that his father did like me. Clint said that is how his father shows his love to you; he aggravates the people he loves. I didn't really understand that logic; but if Clint said it, then it must be true.

So we got married and moved into a cute little one-bedroom house off Cane Run Road. Life was so good! I finally had a house of my own. I had a husband who loved me and I loved him.

We both worked hard to make a good life for ourselves. Life was good for about four years, and then I wasn't happy anymore. I was missing something but I didn't know what it was. I also thought I was being controlled. I couldn't do what I wanted to do. I always had to ask permission. *Was this what married life was like? Did the man have all the control in the house?* I know it says that in the Bible, but I think I should have been able to make some decisions on my own.

I was content with the way my life was going. I got to do things that I didn't do growing up like camping, going on a vacation and always having food in the house.

Clint was meeting my wants but I felt like he was not giving me what I needed. I needed more love. The love was not as strong as it once was. I wanted more.

Clint and I did have some good times like when we went to Land Between the Lakes National Recreation Area and we stayed at Bacon Creek. I loved camping, even when it was very primitive and, having no bathroom, we had to bathe in the lake. I must say that using the lake for a bath was a lot better than some of the houses I have lived in.

I tried really hard to be happy. I would go through days when I was happy and then days when I didn't like the person who was staring back at me in the mirror.

As a wife to Clint, I really didn't have a right to complain. Clint was a very hard worker. Sometimes he would work two jobs. One time he was working for a man named Joseph on the side and surprised me with a kidney-shaped coffee table. Joseph helped him bring it home then said to me, "How come every time your husband works for me, you get something new?" I answered, "I don't know, but I like it."

The coffee table was awesome and it was sturdy enough for me to dance on. Yes, you heard me right! To this day, I still like dancing on some kind of platform. I know that this is because of my childhood. My mother was proud of me a long time ago and I wanted to remember that day. So whenever I was feeling down, I would turn up the music and dance.

CHAPTER 7

Having Children

I thought that if I had a baby, the baby would give me the love I needed. I would give that baby love and in return it would love me with an unconditional love. Clint didn't want children and was not happy when I became pregnant. He didn't talk to me for two days after I told him I was pregnant. But I was so happy. I was going to have a baby! The house that we were living in was small with only one bedroom. That was okay. We could make it work. This baby would make a difference in my life and in my husband's.

At the time, I think I was driving Clint crazy. All I talked about was baby, baby, and baby. When the baby was growing inside of me, I would talk and sing to it. I had heard and read that the baby will know your voice if you talk to it. I hoped my singing wouldn't make my baby tone deaf, however I sang anyway. I would lie on the floor to get the baby to move. The way it felt for me was like a butterfly. I think I drove the baby crazy, too, because the last month I wasn't feeling the baby move. I felt like I had done something wrong.

So then I started reading again, all I could. I ended up calling my doctor and his nurse said it was normal. They said the baby was getting settled to be born. Whew, I really didn't want to mess this up.

Clint was not at home much anymore because he was helping his mother with his father. His father had a heart attack and died, but there were two men who stopped to help and got him breathing again. But it was too late for his brain. Clint's father was without oxygen so long that he had some brain damage. So Clint had to help his mother every night. His sisters helped, too.

I thought having a baby would help fill the void in my life and she did. We had a baby girl and if I didn't believe in a God, I did then. She was perfect and I was so proud of her. I would not be the mother that I had. I would tell my daughter every day how much I loved her. My daughter was the only granddaughter on Clint's side, so she would be loved by many others, too.

Having Renae was the greatest thing that had happened to me. I gave her love and, in return, she gave me love. She was with me all the time that I was not working. I couldn't wait until I got off work to go and get her. She was my life. I then began to notice a change in my husband. Clint, too, was happy with his little girl.

Clint started looking for a bigger house when I became pregnant, so we moved into our second house after I had the baby. Renae was three months old when we moved. The new house was larger with two bedrooms and a bigger garage. Clint liked that and would work in the garage after he got home. He worked very hard to make money for our family. He also did very nice work. He made counter tops and cabinets, as well as some furniture. Clint had a gift that was given him to make things with his hands. I was proud of Clint for the way he could take a piece of wood and turn it into something beautiful. If it weren't for Clint working so hard, it would have been hard on us having a child. I was also happy we had nice neighbors Mr. Tucker and Betty Lynn who lived across the street from us.

Renae was an answer to my prayers and I was happy with life again...most of the time. There was still the feeling that I wasn't being loved. Why is that? Even though I had a husband, a daughter, and a home, there was still something not right with me. On most days I could deal with it, but I was having thoughts of no value. It seemed like I had to do everything to make Clint happy. I thought marriage was 50/50. But it was not.

Then when Renae was having her second birthday, I found out that I was pregnant. I was happy and, again, Clint was not. From the time I became pregnant with my second child, I had trouble. This was not like the first. I knew this had to be a boy.

Two days before I had the baby, Renae broke her arm by falling off our bed. It was late and I was tired, so Clint put Renae in bed with us. We were playing with her and she was laughing. Then she went down to the end of the bed, stood up and fell off. Renae hit the floor with one arm behind her back. She landed on one of those toy baby bottles that had the pretend milk in it. The scream was horrible! I jumped up and Clint picked her up. I was running through the house like a crazy woman. Clint was trying to get me to change into some clothes. At one point, he looked at me and told me that if I didn't hurry and get my shoes on, he would leave me there. I hurried! There was no way my daughter was going to the hospital without me. Clint ran so many red lights on the way to the hospital that I was amazed we didn't get into a wreck.

Renae had a broken arm. The nurses and doctor were worried about me because I was stressed and it looked like I could go into labor any minute. The fear of not knowing what was happening to our daughter was awful. I know that the doctors have to tell you the worst case scenario, but hearing that our daughter had broken her arm right in a location where she may not be able to use it again scared me to death. I was praying to God that He would take care of her. They called in a specialist. The specialist was nice and assured us that she would be okay. They gave her some medicine to ease her pain and it made her sleep, which was a good thing.

We were able to take Renae home after they wrapped her arm. We were told that she would need to have it wrapped like this for 4 to 6 weeks. When we got home, we called Clint's family and told them what happened. Everyone was upset because we hadn't called them earlier. Clint didn't want to call anyone. He didn't want to bother anyone. But it's my opinion that if you are having trouble or going through something, you need support. Clint was my husband and he insisted I needed to do what *he* decided was best for our family.

Clint did call Joe who he worked with, and Joe and his wife Lana came down after they got off work that afternoon. We had become good friends with Joe and Lana and went camping together. They were great to both of us.

The next day, I had a really bad headache and had to go to the doctor. My doctor said that I could go into labor any time now and that I should get ready to go to the hospital in a day or two.

Lana and Joe came over that evening and we got Tumbleweed, but I just felt so bad with the headache that I could barely eat. After supper, I talked Clint into letting me go to the hospital. Lana went with me and they told me I was not in labor. The hospital staff informed me that my doctor was in Lagrange and wouldn't be back in Louisville until much later. They sent me home and told me to come back if my headache got worse. Clint was not happy that I went. He was tired and grouchy. Joe and Lana decided to stay all night with us because the nurse told Lana and me before we left that she thought I would be back.

At midnight, I was on the back step drinking hot tea. The headache was so bad. I tried lying down with Renae but even closing my eyes hurt, so I thought the tea would help. Lana came out and sat with me on the back steps. I told her I wanted to go to the hospital again but I didn't want to make Clint mad. She told me to go tell Clint that I was hurting again and ask if he would take me. If not, she would take me. So I went and told Clint that I needed to go back again. He got up, but he was not happy.

"This is your third time going. Can't you just wait until morning?"

"No, I can't wait."

As I was walking down the hallway to get my shoes, my water broke. I yelled at Clint to let him know my water had broken and now they would keep me at the hospital. He went crazy trying to get everything. I guess he knew that I needed to go to the hospital. Again, Clint drove like a wild man and got me to the hospital in record time.

The nurse remembered me and said that she would be there with me until I had the baby. With Renae, we had a whole lot of people but with this baby, Clint only wanted the two of us there. It didn't take long for the baby to come into the world. We had a son! He was so cute. I thought at the time: *Now, I have a perfect family!*

Clint didn't want any more children so he decided that I needed to get my tubes tied. After about 10 minutes with the baby, they took me up to surgery to have a tubal ligation.

Around eight or so, my mother-in-law and Jamie arrived at the hospital. They were a little upset because they had not been called. I told them both that it was not my decision.

Since Renae was at home with a broken arm, I convinced my doctor to let me go home the next day. Renae needed me and I wanted to be there. She was very happy with her baby brother. Renae and Mikey added so much to my life. They became the reason I would get up in the morning. They were everything to me. At times I put them before Clint. Sometimes that is the only thing that got me through the hard days of being married to a man who controlled my life.

When Mikey was about six months old, I became really depressed. All of my adult life, I had been on medication for depression. I think it was because of my past. Then sometimes I would think I didn't need the medication because I was feeling better. But when Mikey was six months old, the doctor said that I had post-partum depression so I was put back on medication. The doctor put me on Prozac. It was working and I was on it for a while.

Clint told his buddies from work that I was feeling better because I went to the doctor and got some medicine. They asked him what the doctor put me on. When Clint came home that night, he asked me if I remembered that day when a man started shooting at Standard Gravure, when there were eight people killed. I told him yes. Clint then told me he had heard that the man who did the shooting was on the same medicine I was taking.

The next day, Clint and his friends at work decided that I didn't need to take that medicine, so Clint threw it in the garbage. It only took about a week without the Prozac for me to sink back into depression. Clint was not helping. It seemed to me that he was on me about everything.

One day I was so proud that I had cleaned the house and taken great care of Renae and Mikey. I even had supper cooking when Clint came in from work. I knew he would be happy that I had taken care of everything. However, I was wrong. Clint did say the house looked good, but he wanted to know why I didn't clean off the top of the refrigerator. *Really, are you kidding me? Who looks at the top of the refrigerator? Not me.*

So, again I felt like a failure, just as my mother used to say. I didn't like it when I couldn't get the comments from my mother out of my head.

That night Clint and I got into a big fight. I was so tired of feeling like a failure over and over. I just couldn't do anything right. I went into the bathroom and took my pain pills for my headache. How many I don't know. I went back in the kitchen and Clint was still on my case. I told him that it will be alright soon.

"What do you mean by that?"

"I am so tired of not being the wife you want and
need, so I am going to check out of this life,"

Clint went to the bathroom and saw that my medicine
bottle was empty. He asked me if I took more than I
needed. I only said, "Time will tell." Clint called his sister
Jamie who lived right around the corner and she came
over.

Jamie asked me what I took. I told her I can't do it
anymore, so I took a whole lot. She went into our bedroom
and called the hospital. Jamie worked at the hospital so
she called one of her friends, who told her I needed to go
to the hospital. Jamie came back into the kitchen where
Clint and I were still yelling at one another. I was at the
sink and Clint was telling Jamie all I did and didn't do as a
wife.

I think something must have clicked and I went off.
I grabbed a knife and turned around and told Clint to quit
talking like I wasn't even there. I didn't try to stab him, as
I knew he was a lot stronger than I was. Clint took the knife
and slapped me across the face. I think he really thought
that if he slapped me, I would come to my senses.

Clint told me that I either let him drive me to the
hospital or he was calling the police. So I thought of Renae
and Mikey who were asleep in the other room and told him
I would go with him. All the way to the hospital, Clint went
on and on telling me that if I would just do what he said,
we wouldn't fight. I didn't say a word.

At the hospital, I got to go back by myself. For that, I was relieved. I told the doctor all that was going on and that I had dealt with depression all my life. I also told him that I had a baby six months ago and explained how Clint and his friends decided I didn't need to be on my depression medicine due to a shooting where people got killed. To say the least, that doctor went to talk to Clint.

I had to stay all night. I had to have someone stay with me because I had tried to take my own life. However, I didn't want Clint there. So, I called Sheila and she came to sit with me. At some point, Joe came by to make sure I was okay. His wife Lana was sick and didn't come. I told Joe I was going to be fine.

I was released the next day and the doctor put me on a different medicine. He also told me to never quit taking the medicine on my own. He said that if I was going off it, I needed to be under a doctor's care.

When I went home, it was quiet. Clint even started to help. At that moment, I knew things would be better for a time. However, I didn't know how long it would last.

The medicine helped get me back to a place where I could cope with things, and I felt like I was needed and wanted. Clint never tried to mess with my medicine again. I found out that the doctor really chewed him out and even asked him sarcastically, "What medical school did you go to?" The doctor told him that if he didn't have a medical license, then he couldn't be a doctor. I wished I could have been there to witness it. Although I wasn't, I had a good idea that Clint didn't like it.

To me it seemed that we were both trying to do better. Yet sometimes I still felt as though Clint was on me all the time. On the other hand, Clint treated my father with so much respect. Clint was taught to respect his elders.

My Aunt Delores and father got a divorce. My father was still living in the house he built. I would call him at least every other day to check on him. The phone calls would be short because he was still a man of few words.

I learned more about my father when he would come to our house. He would tell Clint things while they were out in the garage. Then Clint would tell me what they talked about. I was happy my father was talking to my husband.

One day I got a call that my father was at Jewish Hospital and I needed to get there quickly. When I got there, I was told that my father had just had a stroke. The nurse then told me that she had my father's things and I needed to sign for them.

So, I signed for them. She said, "Ma'am, your father had a lot of money on him. Please be careful." I looked in the envelope and there was a huge wad of money. The nurse said, "It was in his front pants pocket." I told her, "I know my father doesn't like banks." I thanked the nurse and she said she would call me when it was okay to see him.

When I went back to see my father, I cried. Since finding out that he was my father, I thought he hung the moon. The doctor came and told me that my father had suffered a stroke. He had a trach now and that there wasn't much on the EEG, or brain scan.

When I learned that I did have a father at fifteen, I also found out that I had two step-sisters and one step-brother. So I called all of them and told them about our father. I did go get paperwork at the court house so I could make decisions for my father. I also put a do-not-resuscitate order on my father because of what the doctors were saying about his EEG.

Grace, who lived in New York City, called the hospital to check on our father and found out I had put a do-not-resuscitate order on him. She then asked the hospital to take the order off and said that she would be there as soon as she could get a flight out. I had never met Grace before and when she walked in to the hospital, you would have thought she was the Queen of England. I know that was not a very nice thought, but that was the way she acted.

Grace did shake my hand and told me that she wanted to talk to our father alone. I said that was ok with me. Grace did have some people with her, but she didn't introduce them to me. They went back with her, too.

As I sat in the waiting room, I prayed to God that no matter what was going on in the room, my father was at peace and wasn't afraid. I had heard that Grace was going to give our father a piece of her mind. When they came out,

Grace walked over and told me that she put the do-not-resuscitate order back on. Then she was out the door as fast as she came in.

I went back and sat with my father for a while. I held his hand and talked to him, saying, "I wish I had known you were my father when I was little. I don't know if I would have told you what I was going through as a child. However, I want you to know that I prayed every night that if my father was alive that he would know that he was loved by me." When I left that evening, I had a very heavy heart. It felt like I was losing my father. When I reached home that night, Clint already had the children in bed and he asked, "How is your father?" I said, "The same."

My father stayed in the hospital until they transported him to a nursing home in Evansville, Indiana, on August 20th. Renae and I followed the ambulance that transported him there. Well, let me rephrase that. I *tried* to follow the ambulance. They drove too fast.

When we got to the nursing home, my father was already in a room. I had to sign some papers before going to his room. Renae, who was just four, was good as gold. I told her that when we were done, I would take her to McDonald's.

After I put some things in my father's room, I went over and took his hand and said, "Daddy, I love you. I will be back on Saturday to see you." When I said that, my father opened his eyes. Not once in Jewish Hospital had my father opened his eyes. I was excited at first, but when I talked to my father it was like I was talking to a blank stare. I talked to the nurse and she said that happens sometimes. I told him again that I loved him then we left.

I took Renae to McDonald's then we were on the road again to go home. I was happy to have Renae with me and that we had a little mother-daughter time together.

I was not prepared for the call I received on August 22nd. It was a woman from the nursing home.

"I really hate to tell you over the phone, but your father has expired."

"Excuse me?"

"Your father has expired."

By then, Clint was standing right by me. I told the lady I didn't understand.

"Your father died."

Well, I knew what that meant and I lost it. I had never heard someone tell a daughter that her father has expired before. I said one more thing to that lady:

"Lady, my father is not spoiled milk."

Then I just sat on the bed and bawled like a baby. Clint took the phone and talked with the lady at the nursing home. Clint made the phone calls that needed to be made. He was my rock when I needed him the most.

I didn't know how I was going to get my father's body back from Indiana. I knew my father didn't have any insurance. One of my cousins called me and told me that since my father was a resident of Kentucky, the state of Kentucky would bring him back.

The next day, I went downtown and talked to a very nice man about my father and how I could get him buried. He told me that they had a cemetery where my father could be buried without insurance. However, he stressed to me that it would be very simple. He said I couldn't order programs or flowers for a casket because if we could do all the extra things that go with a funeral, then we could pay for the funeral.

"How much would it cost to bury my father in the cemetery?"

"Six hundred and seventy five dollars."

I then told him that my father had a small house and when I sold it, I would be back to pay him the money. He assured me that would be great and I signed a paper saying I would pay the state back for the funeral. Before I got up to leave, I reached over and shook the man's hand and said, "Thanks for being here for my father and allowing me to bury my father." The man's reply was a blessing from God:

"Your father would be proud of you for taking care of him in his final days. I will pray for you and your family."

I don't know how I made it home. I didn't know I had so many tears to shed. I was sad because my father passed away, and I was happy to hear from a total stranger that my father would be proud of me. To me that was a wink from God that He was with me.

The funeral was very simple. All my sisters and brothers and step-sisters and step-brother came. After spending some time with Grace, Becky and Mason, I realized that Grace, who acted like the Queen of England, was not bad at all. When she had come to the hospital, she had to do what was best for her at the time. I was happy that I got to see a different side of Grace. There were also uncles and one aunt who came from my father's side of the family. I had the Garth Brooks song, *The Dance,* played at his funeral. Then everyone went to the cemetery. That didn't last long either. Afterwards, we invited everyone back to our house to eat.

We had food from everywhere, family, friends church members and our neighbors Mr. Tucker and Ms. Betty Lynn. I couldn't believe everyone help me get through one of my worst days. I think everyone did have a good time talking to everyone. I was happy that we opened our doors for my father's family and that we took pictures with all the brothers and sisters.

Clint even made a headstone out of wood for my father's grave. He carved my father's name and the dates. I was so proud of Clint for doing that for my father and me.

My negative feelings started again when Renae and Mikey were about five and three. There was something not right about my marriage. I kept thinking it was me.

Clint said one day that he thought it was time for us to move. So we started looking for another house. This would be my third house. It didn't take us long to find a big house in Valley Station. It had two garages. One garage could be a place to store his boat and the other one where he could have a shop. The house also had a basement. This was great for me because I could have a sewing room. I had to sew in the kitchen before and I always had to put everything away at night. Clint didn't want anything left out. Sometimes it was a pain to stop and put it up, and then in the morning I would have to drag it all out again. Renae and Mikey were happy, too, because they would have their own rooms.

Yet, in the back of my mind, I still was not happy. I was trying to make the best of my life. I knew I wouldn't be able to continue attending Rockford Lane Baptist church because of the drive back and forth, so for a while I just stayed at home and tried to get the house in order.

Clint worked hard then when he got home and would go to the garage to work. Having two garages was great, but one day it was weird...or could they have been haunted?

On that one odd day, Clint was working on a job in the big garage when he heard the little garage door go up.

He went around and confirmed that the door to the little garage was indeed up. Then Clint came in the side door to our house and asked, "Darlene are you needing something from the little garage?" I said no. Clint closed the door behind him and went back to work.

It wasn't twenty minutes later when I heard the door to the small garage going back up. I also heard Clint pushing the garage door to make it go back down. He came back in and said, "Darlene this is not funny. I have to get the job done." I had not touched the garage door opener! I explained that I was trying to get supper on the table.

Clint went back out to the big garage a third time. When I was almost done with supper, he came in the house again, this time really upset. He said:

"Darlene, I don't know why you are messing with me."

"I am not messing with you!"

When Clint went out the door this time, he slammed it. He was mad as a hornet!

I was sitting the dinner table when Clint walked in with a smile on his face. I asked what happened. "I am sorry," Clint said. The whole time the remote for the little garage was in my pocket and every time I bent over, the door opened. We both started laughing.

Renae and Mikey heard us laughing and came upstairs to see what was so funny. Clint told the story about the mysterious garage door and all four of us laughed together. Clint kissed me and said, "I am sorry. I will go turn off the saw and come back in to clean up for supper."

Laughing is so good for the soul and when we laughed out loud, I made a mental note to write it in my journal so I can read it when I am having a sad or difficult day.

On most nights, if I wanted to talk to Clint, I would have to go outside to the garage. We would eat dinner, then he would go help his mother and then come back home. I began to resent how Clint helped his family. Sure, I knew that it was me being selfish on my part. However, I didn't feel like I was high on his list.

The resentment I felt was because I was at home with Renae and Mikey all the time. I wanted and needed adult conversation with Clint. I wanted him to think of me first. I know I wasn't first on my mother's list. How could I be when there were five other children before me?

When things weren't going right, I would blame myself thinking that I was the one who had the problem. My self-doubts were confirmed when I asked Clint to go with me to a counselor to talk about things. Clint said, "I won't go. I don't have a problem—you do."

CHAPTER 8

Controlled

I wasn't really sure what a real married life should look like, because I had only seen one first-hand for just a short time. I didn't get to see day-in and day-out what a family should be like.

I did witness for a short time the way the Allen's got along and the way they were a family, but that was mostly on Sunday's after church. Even on TV, the family shows like *The Waltons* and *Little House on the Prairie* showed me that families stuck together.

My married life didn't resemble that kind of life. Clint wanted things his way. I was told by someone that if you don't want to be controlled for the rest of your married life, then don't start out that way. I learned that the person who gave me that wisdom was so correct. I wished I would have taken her advice.

Early in our marriage, I was working at an auto parts store and brought home a paycheck every week. But the money went into a joint checking account; and I had to ask for everything. I did get $10.00 a week for spending and I did have gas in the car. Having $10.00 was not really enough to do anything with.

When I would go to the grocery store, Clint didn't like it because I spent too much money. I would end up having a headache before I got home. I liked it when he went to the store with me because I didn't get a headache.

Later on in our marriage after we had Renae and Mikey, I would charge the food because I was too scared to go home with a food bill that Clint didn't like. It got so bad that I signed up for WIC. We qualified for it. However I could never tell Clint what I had done. He didn't want us to ask for help. So when I bought a lot of food, I began to hide it or give it to my friends who needed it.

I knew how it was to be hungry as a child and I wasn't going to let my children have the same feeling of hunger. So I did what I thought a mother should do—provide for her children.

When I laid down at night and I would say my prayers and talk to God, I would tell God that I knew what I was keeping from Clint was wrong. I struggled with honoring my husband. I struggled with keeping secrets again. Over the years, I prayed this prayer:

Dear God,

Please help me understand what I should and should not be doing. Please help me make Clint love me more and not to only see my mistakes.

In Jesus' name,

Amen.

Over the years, I also got into trouble for many things. I couldn't go to a used clothing store and buy things for Renae and Mikey. I had to have things done before Clint got home from work. I had a list of things to do daily. I had to have dinner ready, or at least a plan, before he got home.

I liked going camping and on vacations because Clint acted differently. He was fun and he did silly things with Renae and Mikey. Clint said it was his family tradition that the first time you went in your hotel room, everyone got on the beds and jumped up and down on them. So, we continued that tradition.

On one vacation trip to Florida, Clint and Mikey were out in the ocean. They were having fun when a big wave hit both of them. Clint had worn his glasses in the ocean. When he came up, no glasses! I put my head down in the book I was reading and acted like I hadn't seen what just had happened.

Clint got out of the ocean and Mikey was following behind him. He sat down by me and said, "I lost my glasses in the ocean." To say the least, he was mad as a hornet. My first reaction was to laugh out loud. But, I knew better. I asked:

"What are you going to do without your glasses?"

"I guess we will have to find an eye place."

"They have to be out there."

"Darlene, they are long gone."

"Well, I am going to go look again." I turned around and asked, "If I find them what do I get?"

"I tell you what you will get. I will buy you that glass alligator you were looking at."

So, I turned around and went back into the ocean. I was out there for about ten minutes and as I was moving my toes around in the sand, I said this prayer:

God, I know you see me down here looking for a pair of glasses in your ocean. Could you help me find them, please?

The very instant I ended the prayer, my toe hit something and I reached down and picked up the pair of glasses. *YES! I have a big God.* I screamed at the top of my lungs. "I found them, I found them!" Clint couldn't believe I had found the glasses. He was so happy!

At bedtime, Mikey asked me, "How do you think you found Daddy's glasses?" I explained, "I know God found your daddy's glasses and put them where I would find them." Mikey said his prayers while I was by his side:

"Thank you God for helping my mommy find my daddy's glasses and for my mommy's big toe. Amen"

I smiled at Mikey when he opened his eyes and told him, "I love you."

I went over to Renae's side of the bed and asked, "Did you say your prayers?" She said, "I just said the same thing Mikey said, but I didn't say you had a big toe. My brother says the silliest things." I gave her a hug and said, "Yes he does," and told her, "I love you."

When I went back into the other room, Clint was watching a basketball game and I told him what Renae and Mikey had said about me finding Daddy's glasses.

"I couldn't believe you found them, thanks."

"I can't wait to tell our family that I found your glasses. No one will believe us!"

We both just laughed and finished watching the basketball game. It was a nice evening we both had, and I was happy.

The next day, I was on the balcony reading a book and drinking coffee. Clint asked why I looked so sad.

"Because we have to go back home."

"I know, but we will come back again."

As I was packing up the things to go home, I talked to God and told him I wished that our everyday life could be like this vacation. We were a happy family on vacation. We got along and there was no sadness.

As we drove home, Clint and I discussed me going back to work. I was looking forward to it because it was way too quiet at home when Renae and Mikey were in school and Clint was at work. Plus, there is only so much housework you can do.

With Renae and Mikey both starting school, I started back to work. I was working as an assistant in a pre-school classroom. I got the opportunity because I had worked in a mother's-day-out program when my children were small. I had also had experience working in a daycare, but had to quit that job because Mikey was so sick that we went into the red one month.

Working in the classroom and being around other adults was what I was craving. I needed and wanted adult conversation. It was there that I learned that I didn't have an ideal marriage. The co-workers thought I was odd because I had to rush home as soon as I finished work to get the things done from the list before Clint made it home right after. I confided in them what it was like in our house, and they shared with me what their life was like. I was not being treated like a wife.

With this new awareness, I started changing. Changes are good for people who want to make a difference and don't want to be controlled by others. For the person who doesn't want change, however, it is very hard. This caused more fights and resentment for both of us.

CHAPTER 9

Getting Divorced

One day Clint was out in what we called the *hot room*. It was a room added on to the back of the house in which we had a hot tub. It was a nice place to be when you needed some time alone. I went and sat down at the table and we were just making small talk. Clint looked at me and asked, "Do you still want a divorce?"

At that moment, I didn't really know what to say. If I said the wrong thing, it could be bad for me. I, in return, answered a question with a question, "What do you want?"

"I think it is time that we do get a divorce. I also need to tell you that I closed the savings account in our name. The money in that account was mine and you are not entitled to it."

I started getting mad at that point and said:

"I thought that was the account that I opened up. I know that most of that money is yours because it is the money you got after your mother passed away. But, there is money in there that was ours."

"The money that was in there is the money I put in from the side jobs that I have."

"Then, yes, I want a divorce. Because you will never change and I want out."

When I went to bed that night, I was so confused. I was happy, but sad, too. It would be hard telling Renae and Mikey and...*where would I go?*

The next day, I contacted a lawyer and made an appointment. Our meeting was set for the following week. So, I started making a list of what I needed to do.

At work, they weren't surprised that I was going to get a divorce because they knew I was unhappy, even though I had told them that Clint would never give me a divorce. He told me more than once that he wouldn't give me half of what he worked so hard for. However when his mother passed away just a few years after his father, it was like he didn't have to live up to their expectations any more.

When Clint came home the next few days, I would go out in the garage and ask him questions like, "How are we going to do this? Are we going to be like our friends who got a divorce and are always fighting?" Clint said it wouldn't be like that. We would put the children first. There would be no fighting over things. He said, "You can take anything in the house except for my parent's bedroom suite."

The day we told Renae and Mikey was one of my hardest days. We waited until after supper and we sat at the dining room table.

Renae started crying because she didn't want us to fight like our friends. We assured her that we wouldn't. Mikey didn't say a whole lot. We told them that we would both have them and that they weren't going to lose a mother or a father. It broke my heart. However, inside there was a spark of hope. I will be happy one day.

Over the next couple of weeks, I was busy. I went to the lawyer and learned the details of what I needed to do. He said because we have children, we would have to go to class before the judge would grant us a divorce. Well, I thought right then that the divorce thing would be over, because Clint wouldn't go for that.

I had papers that needed to be filled out and then Clint would be served. Even though we were getting a divorce, we were still talking and sleeping in the same bed. I was still doing what Clint told me to do.

Clint decided that we would have one lawyer so we wouldn't have to pay for two. He decided that he wouldn't pay child support because we would split the time with the children evenly. Clint would have Renae and Mikey for seven days and I would have them the next seven days. He said he will supply Renae and Mikey with everything they need. I thought that would be okay, because Clint had never lied to me. I trusted Clint, even if I was going to divorce him.

I started packing and looking for a place to live. Clint said I couldn't live in a trailer. So, I asked where I could live. He said that he would check wherever I decided to move to before signing the papers.

My work friends, Michelle, Ms. Pat and Christina, thought I was crazy for using the same lawyer as Clint, for allowing him to tell me where I was going to live, and for not getting child support. I explained to them that Clint had never lied to me. They said that would change before the divorce was over.

Clint and I did meet with the lawyer together. The attorney said he could work for both of us. He would take extra steps to make it fair for both of us. I then learned that Clint would have to pay me some money because we had been married for sixteen years. How much would depend on the amount of the sale of the house we owned. From that day on, I didn't look at apartments. I started looking at houses.

Renae and Mikey were doing better and I would take them to look at the houses I was interested in buying. We found a house that wasn't too far from their father's. It would be close enough for them to walk if they wanted to. They could still go to the same school from both addresses.

So the day came when Clint came to inspect the house. He walked throughout the house and, when he reached the master bedroom, he turned to me and said, "You can't afford this house." Renae and Mikey were so excited because they would be close to both of us.

The very next day, I went and applied for a loan on that very house. I wanted that house. It was just what we needed. Plus, I was divorcing this man. He was not going to tell me where I was going to live.

With the money Clint had to give me, I could afford the house. However, it wasn't going to be easy. Then again, up to this point, my life had never been easy.

I also started looking for a second job. I thought I could do this since I would need something to do when Renae and Mikey were staying at their father's for seven days. I got a job at a gas station that was not far from the house. I started right away. Clint said to me, "I am proud of you for getting a second job," and, "You know it won't be easy." I replied, "My life has never been easy."

I also moved my things to the basement. I was divorcing this man so I didn't have to sleep with him. We were still getting along which helped Renae and Mikey.

We started packing things. This was so much easier than I thought it would be. Clint had to refinance the house to pay me what the lawyer said he had to pay according to the law. He was not happy because he had to pay a higher rate because of our credit score. Would you believe he blamed me and said it was entirely my fault? Well, that was no change...Clint always blamed me for everything.

I then went to the loan office and told them I had the money for my down payment. Plus, I had money to buy the things I needed for the new house. Clint also agreed to give me ten percent of the amount he earned from his side jobs. I thought that was fair and that I could set aside the money in a savings account for emergencies.

Everything was coming together and I was going to move out on November 22nd, which would be the day before Thanksgiving. I was so excited that I was going to have my very own house. Words can't describe how I felt when I received the keys to my house. I felt happy, sad, excited and scared all at once!

Clint and I had been married for sixteen years. Even in the end, Clint was still trying to provide what I needed. I took everything that I thought I should take for the children. I left Renae's bedroom furniture because Clint had made it. I left Mike's chest because Clint didn't make junk, so he didn't make the furniture light.

My living room furniture and Renae and Mikey's bedroom furniture was being delivered on the 22nd, so I was going to sleep in the house that night. Renae and Mikey wanted to sleep there, too, on the first night. We had to ask permission from their father. That is when we started the seven days when the children would be at my house. *Whew, it was finally happening!*

Thanksgiving Day was just another day for me that year. I was going to be moving all my things to my house the very next day. Clint and our good friend, Joe, were going to move everything the next day. Yes, that's right. Clint was moving me out. There were no harsh words. We were still getting along.

Moving day went great, and it didn't take long either. If I didn't know where I wanted things to go, they just went to the garage. I told Mikey that when things got settled, he could have the garage as his own. It was a one-car garage.

When the final truck was unloaded, I thanked Clint and Joe, then they left my driveway. I considered Clint my soon-to-be ex. All the papers were signed and the divorce papers would soon be coming in the mail. I was not under his control anymore. That gave me a great feeling.

It was great getting the house together. I didn't really have to do much to the house. The man who had lived there had passed away, however, he had kept the house repairs up. The only thing I needed to do was clean everything. We took our time moving things in from the garage. It was nice that there was no stress in the house.

At this point in my life, I did what I wanted to do. I didn't have to answer to anyone.

We got a lot done during the first week Renae and Mikey were with me. Clint called every day at 9:00 p.m. If Renae and Mikey wanted to call their father, they could at any time.

When the children left for school that Wednesday, I knew that they wouldn't be back to my house for seven days. I acted as though I was fine when they were getting ready to leave. I wrote this poem on paper for them. I told them not to read it until they got to their father's house, and if and when they ever started to miss me to read the note. I gave each of them a kiss and the biggest hug.

> Renae and Mike,
> children of mine.
> I love the both of you,
> from the beginning of time.
> Even though your
> Dad and I are not
> Together anymore,
> The both of you,
> are loved and adored.

I watched as they walked to their bus stop. I was still smiling when they looked back at me, however I was sick inside. *What am I going to do without Renae and Mikey?* Over the years, I have only been away from them for short periods of time. I assured them that I would call at nine and they could call me at any time.

I had my children at school to teach and my job at the gas station. I knew I wanted to sew some things for the house. I also wanted to go out dancing. So on Thursday, I went to work and made plans with Michelle to go out on Friday, since I didn't have to work that coming Friday evening.

It wasn't easy the first week and even the next few times that it was their father's week. However, I worked very hard to stay busy while Renae and Mikey were gone. Michelle and Ms. Pat helped me a lot. They also laughed at me because whenever they drove by my house, every light was on. I think there is a country song that says those very same words. See, my life could be a country song.

It was scary when Renae and Mikey were gone. I even slept in the living room. I kept telling myself that in time it would get better.

The day that Clint brought Renae and Mikey home, he also brought food for them, as well, and other supplies that they needed. Somehow, this didn't feel right because he was still in control even though it was my house. Clint also gave them lunch money for the week, which he made me sign a receipt for. Other than that, Clint was still keeping his word.

One thing we did was to keep Renae and Mikey in church. Whether I went to church or not, the children were taken to church. I even joined a Divorce Care class, which helped because I found out some of the things I thought were my fault really weren't.

The day I got my divorce papers was a sad day, because on that day I felt like a failure. I could just hear the echoes of my mother's voice. "Clint won't stay with you long. You are a piece of garbage. You're used goods." I wanted so much to say, "Yes, because it was your boyfriend who molested me and raped me." But I didn't. This conversation happened after I got married when I went to see my mother one day. I always wanted to feel loved by her. I was always searching to find a way to make her proud of me.

That night I went out and, to say the least, celebrated too much. It was the first time I can say I got drunk. The next day, I told myself I would never do that again. I don't understand how people do that day in and day out.

I think that, over all, Renae, Mikey and I were adjusting fairly well. Even on Christmas Day, their father came over to watch Renae and Mikey open presents. It didn't start out very good for Clint because when he turned into my driveway, he cut the tire too close causing it to hit this metal thing that sliced it. I must say I thought it was funny. However, Clint did not. That was the only Christmas we got together like that, and I am thankful that we could do it for the children.

Something was changing with our new routine. However, I had the feeling in my gut that Clint was still in charge even though I had moved out.

I learned very early that being a single mother is no easy task. It was so hard at times. There were times that I didn't know if I was making the right decisions. But I did like the freedom to make my own choices, and just knowing that I wouldn't get yelled at or in trouble as an adult was a good feeling.

I came and went as I pleased. Sure, I had Renae and Mikey to look after, but everything was different.

My job as a Pre-Kindergarten teacher was a great place for me to be. I felt important, needed and even loved. I got to go to work early and stay late if I wanted to. On the week that I didn't have my children, I did just that. I didn't like going home alone.

On a few Friday nights, I would go out dancing. Could I dance? No. But I always had a good time. I wasn't much of a drinker. I was finding that some freedoms needed to be watched closely.

I danced with men who I didn't know. All of them were nice. At the end of the night, I went home alone. I didn't need to bring a man home. I had just gotten out of a marriage. I liked the freedom that I had.

For three months I enjoyed my "me time." However, there came a time that I didn't like being alone. Yes, I said it. I started to feel as though I needed a man in my life.

CHAPTER 10

The Man of my Dreams

I was ready to date. Diana, a co-worker at my school, told me one day that when I was ready to date, she had someone she wanted me to meet. I asked a lot of questions. I learned he had two boys and lived in the neighborhood of the school. So on January 19th, I went on a blind date.

Diana gave Johnny my name and address. I wasn't scared of him picking me up at my house because Diana said he was a good guy. I was sitting on the couch listening to the song *One More Day* by Diamond Rio when he knocked on the door. I let him in and asked if he wanted to sit down. He said sure.

"I guess you know I am Darlene."

"I sure hope so."

I was nervous and I could tell Johnny was, too. I asked him what time we were supposed to meet Jay and Diana. He said at 7:00 p.m. We had a few minutes, so I asked if he wanted a drink. He said no, he was okay. So, we just watched some television. *If You Kiss Me Like That* by Toby Keith came on. I said, "This is a great song," so we listened to it.

When it was over, I asked Johnny if he liked country music. Johnny said that he did, and I said I did and also listened to a little bit of rock. "Are you ready?" Johnny asked. "Sure," I told him. Then I got my coat out of the closet because it was cold outside and there was a little bit of snow remaining from the previous snow fall.

Johnny came around and opened the car door for me. I smiled. I could get used to this. We didn't have very far to go, so we didn't really talk. When we pulled into the parking lot of Mark's Feed Store, he asked me if this was alright. I told him it was great. We sat in the parking lot for a few minutes. Johnny said, "I don't really know if they are here yet. Do you want to go in and see?" I said yes, so we went in and found Jay and Diana at a table up front. We sat with them and made small talk.

I only ordered a little bit because I don't like to eat in front of people. I listened while the others talked. I just wanted to have a good time. After we finished eating, Jay and Diana asked us if we wanted to go to the 19th Hole. It was a bar that had karaoke and was not too far from the restaurant.

Now, I must tell you that my co-workers, Michelle, Pat and Christina, gave me a few pointers about dating since I hadn't been on one in 20 years. Here they are: *Don't kiss on the first date. Don't drink on the first date, and don't sing.* My co-workers know that I can't sing. However, my children who I teach don't. I just told all my coworkers that I could handle myself.

As we were going over to the bar, I smiled while thinking about the conversation I had with my co-workers. Johnny asked me what I was smiling about. I told him I was thinking about something my co-workers discussed with me about going out on my first date.

"Do you want to let me in on it?"

"Not right now, but I am having a great time."

He smiled back and said, "Me too."

It was crowded when we arrived. We found a table close to the dance floor. I asked Johnny, "Do you like to dance?" He said, "I will slow dance but I don't really dance." That was okay with me because I would dance if the right song was played. Johnny asked me if I wanted a drink.

"Sure but I am buying my own."

"No, you are not. I will buy."

"Okay, however, if I want another one I will buy the next time for both of us."

Johnny was agreeable to this, but I could tell he didn't like it. I ordered a piña colada. He ordered a Coke. I looked at him and said, "A Coke?" Johnny replied telling me he doesn't drink. I then asked a very stupid question:

"You don't mind me having one, right?"

"No, not at all."

Well, they started playing the song Electric Slide so I quickly got up to dance. Diana asked me, "What do you think?" I told her it was going well, and that I was having fun. When we got back to the table, I sat down and asked Johnny if he was having fun.

"Yes, I am. Thanks for going on a date with me."

"You are welcome."

I leaned over and kissed Johnny. His lips were so soft, but the kiss didn't last long. However, I could hear my co-workers' "Do Not Do" list in my head. *Oh well, I will tell them I had a great time.* I asked Johnny if it was okay for me to kiss him. He said, "I didn't mind and you can kiss me anytime." I just laughed out loud.

After what seemed like no time at all, we were talking and laughing and having a very good time. Johnny and I danced one slow dance. Johnny can slow dance, but I thought he was a little uncomfortable so I didn't ask him to dance a fast one.

I just had to call Michelle and tell her that I was having fun. I told Johnny that I wanted to call my friend, so I went outside and called Michelle. I told Michelle that I was having fun and that I had already done two of the three things that I wasn't supposed to do.

"What Darlene?"

"Well, I had a few drinks and I kissed him, and I really liked it."

"Darlene be careful."

"I will."

Michelle told me there were four things I wasn't supposed to be doing. But, my phone was beeping when I looked at the screen. It was Renae calling me. I told Michelle I had to get off the phone because Renae was calling.

"Okay, have fun and be careful."

"Okay."

But while I was hanging up I heard her say, "There are four..."

Then I switched over to talk to Renae. "Hi, Honey," I said. I was trying to sound like I was at home, but it was very hard to do because of the noise from inside the bar.

"Are you at home?"

"No, I am out with a friend and I've been dancing."

"Oh."

I told her I was okay, otherwise she would worry about me. After talking to her, she told me Mikey wanted to talk to me. So I talked to him. I asked how he was doing and he told me, "Okay." I told them both that I loved them and would talk to them tomorrow.

After I got off the phone, I felt a bit guilty because I was out having fun. I told Johnny that the call was from my daughter and son and that they called every night at nine. However, tonight it was later because they had gone to a party. He said that was okay, followed by, "I don't get a call every night. Their mother tries to control them while they are away from me."

We went back into the bar and I had one more drink. We stayed for a few more dances; I was happy that I didn't drink enough to get up and sing. I thought to myself that I really liked this freedom to have fun.

We left around midnight and Johnny took me home. I asked if he wanted to come in. I told him that I only had Coke to drink. He said, "Yes, I would love to come in." I took his coat and hung it up, and then told him to make himself at home. I told him I would be right back. I was so happy that this house had two bathrooms. I went to my bathroom and then went back out to the living room.

We talked for hours about each of our past marriages. We each had two children. Johnny had two boys, Scott and Max, who were eight and ten. He also had custody of his boys every other week like I did. So if we dated after tonight, we would have the children at the same time.

When I went to school on Monday, I told Michelle, Christina and Ms. Pat about my date.

"Michelle, you said there are four things I shouldn't do. But, I don't remember the fourth one."

Christina spoke up and said, "Don't shave your legs!" There is a theory that if a woman shaves her legs before going on a date, it means the woman is prepared to have sex if the date goes well. I found this theory very silly. I reassured them:

"Oh, I remembered that was one of the things I shouldn't so. No worries!"

However, I was sure I was going to have another date with Johnny.

I met Johnny on January 19th, dated him just over three months, and married him on April 24th.

Now, there were people in my life who thought that was just too fast. However, I was being treated very well by a man and I wanted to do the right thing. I didn't want to just live with a man because of my children.

At first, everything worked out fine. Johnny and I would have all the children for seven days and then it would be seven days without the children. However, blended families are very hard. The children's ages were 8, 10, 12 and 14. On the days we had all four children, there was a lot of fighting and yelling, in addition to working around our ex's.

We did have fun. Johnny and his boys loved camping and my family loved camping. However, Johnny had a camper and that was different than camping with my ex in a tent. It was so nice going camping and not having to sleep in a tent. We were able to camp at electric spots.

I had a problem, though. I didn't like that Renae, Mikey and I went to church while Scott, Max and Johnny stayed at home. To me, we weren't a family and the fighting and yelling just got worse. So after eight months, I filed for divorce. However, I still loved Johnny.

CHAPTER 11

Dating my Ex

I was still in love with Johnny and I missed him. Yes, I had just divorced him. However, we were so good together when the children weren't around. It was like I was living in heaven for seven days and living in hell the next seven days. We were having trouble only when we had the children, even though we both knew we had children before we married each other.

So, one day out of the blue I got a call from Johnny. He asked me how I was doing because he was doing terrible. I told him that I was doing terrible, too. He wanted to know if I wanted to go and get something to eat. So we started dating. We only dated when we didn't have the children. I decided that I didn't need a piece of paper that said I was married or divorced to have sex with Johnny.

I kept the fact that I was dating Johnny to myself, because I didn't want to hear all my friends and family telling me what I could and couldn't do. It was like I was living two lives. I would be this devoted mother for seven days and do what I was supposed to do. Then for the next seven days, I was the girlfriend of the man I loved. We were playing house every other week. To me, I just thought that I had the perfect life.

One week when I had my children and went to church, I heard Pastor Kevin Hamm preach, "Valley View church is not a hotel for saints. It is a hospital for sinners." *Wow that hurt! Not only did Pastor Kevin step on my toes, he spoke to my heart.*

That night, I got down on my knees and talked to God. I even tried to explain to God why I felt it wasn't a sin. But what I heard was, "Darlene, I love you." As I lay there that night, I knew in my heart why I was trying to convince God that what I was doing was not bad. It was because I wanted to be loved.

I knew I was living wrongly and that I needed to make a decision. So I told Johnny I couldn't live like this anymore. I was burning a candle at both ends. I also mentioned that I had started getting headaches and I wasn't sleeping well. I said, "Johnny, you know I love you, but I can't live like this." That week was the last time I played house.

I had to find something to fill my time, so I got a second job at H & S Hardware. That filled my nights so I could try to forget about Johnny.

Working at H & S hardware store and working at school did make a difference. It filled all my time that needed to be filled, except when my children were with their father. That is when I had the hardest time. That is when I missed Johnny the most. Even though I tried to work two jobs like I did when Renae and Mikey were with me, going home after dark was the worst.

I hated going home by myself. Even though I left all the lights on when I went into my home, I would go to each and every room and look under the bed and in every closet. As always, there was no one in the closet. But I looked anyway. I thought to myself that if someone would have been there when I opened the door, I probably would have had a heart attack.

After everything was checked and I had made sure every window was locked, I could relax. I would then make dinner if I hadn't eaten yet or a snack if I had. I would turn on the TV and watch Hallmark movies or Lifetime movie channel. As long as they didn't have scary movies, I was okay. While Renae and Mikey were gone, I would always sleep on the couch. I hated sleeping in my bedroom when the children were gone.

One afternoon, Johnny and Max came to the hardware store and I even checked him out.

"How are you doing, Darlene?"

"I am doing fine. Some nights are lonely but I am adjusting."

As Johnny was leaving, he turned and said, "I miss you, Darlene." All I did was just smile at him. When he was out the door, I thought to myself that I wished we could have made things work. I was thankful I had another customer to help get my head out of the clouds.

Johnny started visiting me up at the hardware store. One night he said, "Please come and talk to me." So after closing, I went and talked to him.

"I know you won't believe this, Darlene, but I can't live without you. I love you and I know you love me. Please marry me."

"Johnny, it didn't work the first time. I don't want a repeat of all the fights and yelling. Plus, I didn't like the way half the family went to church and the other half stayed home."

"I promise you that things will be different this time. I promise that I will go to church with you. I am willing to do anything to get you back. I love you."

"I will think about it and I will pray about it, and I will talk to my children. I suggest you talk to your children too."

Then Johnny leaned over and kissed me, and I knew that I would be marrying this man again because I loved him.

Talking to Renae and Mikey about marrying Johnny for the second time was a lot easier than I thought it would be. Renae and Mikey just wanted me to be happy. They felt better and didn't have to worry so much about me when I was married. So on February 13th, I remarried Johnny. We had a Justice of the Peace come to Johnny's house and marry us. I wanted to get married on February 13 because the numbers meant something to me. The number two was for two adults, the number one was for one daughter and the number three was for three sons. I even wrote a poem to read at the wedding.

Today started out great,
I woke up early
I didn't sleep late.

I thought of you
And it made me smile.
I am so glad you went
that extra mile.

I don't know what life
Has in store, but it sure
Will be interesting
and we won't be bored.

For we have Renae, Scott
Mikey and Max
To make sure our life is just that.

I will love you tomorrow as
I do today.
For you are in my heart
Forever to stay.

We didn't invite a lot of people to the second wedding. There were some people who just didn't understand why I was getting married a second time to the same man.

This was also the first time that I had a big argument with Michelle. She couldn't understand why I was marrying Johnny again. I said, "Michelle, I love him and he promised me that it will be different this time!" Michelle had no problem voicing her feelings.

"Darlene, if it didn't work the first time, it won't work the second time."

Here is the reason why I did it: I loved Johnny, plain and simple.

Johnny taught me how to do things like skirt a trailer, build a deck and pour concrete. I loved going on jobs with him. If we had the children, Johnny's mom Esther would come and watch them so I could go with Johnny.

Esther was a great mother-in-law and I was happy to have her in my life. While she watched our children, she would clean house if it needed to be done and do the laundry. We always had laundry to do. The second time around was great and lasted longer than the first. I felt very honored when Johnny and his father came to watch Renae and Mikey get baptized. But that was the only time Johnny went to church with me.

Broken promises along with the yelling and screaming just took a toll on me. I told Johnny, "This marriage is not going to work." I tried my best to make it work, but we were too different. Johnny was set in his ways and so was I.

I moved out and had a lot of work ahead of me at my house. I had rented out my house while I was married to Johnny because something in the back of my mind kept saying: *Don't sell the house.* Sometimes it was louder than other times.

I trusted that the renters would take care of my house because they knew me. That was not the case. My house was terrible. It looked like they didn't flush the toilet for the two years that they had been there. In one of the bedrooms, planks were missing under the carpet. I didn't understand why that had happened.

Since I had started going back to church at Valley View and going to the Divorce Care class, I got to talk about what was going in my life. Because I was overwhelmed with all the work that needed to be done, the teacher of the class, Gary, gave me the name of a man who laid carpet. Every bit of the carpet needed to be replaced.

Free advice to everyone reading this: In my opinion, if it doesn't work the first time, chances are it is not going to work the second time.

CHAPTER 12

Adoptive Family

At this point in my life, I had been through three divorces, was starting to attend church regularly and meeting new friends. One special friend became a life line for me. Terry Young introduced me to his family, and in doing so, presented me with the most wonderful gift ever–a second family. This second family consisted of a Mom and Dad, three sisters–Connie who is married to Doug, Kim who is married to Dean, and Tonya who is married to Rick, and two brothers–Michael who is married to Debra and Vic who is married to Diane. Plus there are many others who I loved and appreciated. A note I wrote to Connie on November 2:

> Hi,
>
> I am glad Terry came into my life because he gave me a great friend. Sure we know who the real person to get the praise is: God. But I believe

God gave me Terry as a friend so I would receive the love that I feel with you and your whole family. I know you have many of Noah's items, but this blanket has meaning. I feel the two of us are great friends! Plus, this blanket will keep you warm. Thanks, for always being there for me!!

Love always and forever,
Darlene

The three sisters all had family values. There was a bond between them that was so special. I was proud to be a part of their lives. Each one of the sisters had a special gift. I had the privilege to see each of the sister's gifts.

Connie would help anyone. Sometimes the person doesn't even have to ask. It is like she had a sense that they just needed someone to listen or needed more. Connie also got things done and always called on prayers warriors when needed.

Connie's house was open to anyone. It is kind of like when some children were little there was one house that all the children gather at. That was Connie's house. Most - of the holidays and get-togethers were at Connie's and Doug's house. Connie also made the best meatloaf in the state of Kentucky. Once I asked her, "How do you make your meatloaf so good?" She replied, "A little of this and a dash of that and a lot of Ketchup."

As I watched Connie, I learned so much from her wisdom. She would ask me questions to get me to think and I would ask her questions when I needed help in deciding what to do. I still had to make my own decisions, however it was great to talk to Connie and know I would get an answer. It might not be the answer I was looking for, but it was a true answer. Connie didn't tell you things you wanted to hear; she told you the truth. Sometimes I didn't want to hear the truth. But if I am going to ask anyone a question, I can't expect them to agree with me on everything. I spent most of my time with Connie. She and Doug went to the same church as me, and it was great sitting by them when most of the time I would either sit with my Sunday school class or by myself. When I became part of their family, I knew without a doubt that I would be sitting with family. I don't think Terry knew what a gift he gave me when he introduced me to Connie.

Kim is the sister who lived out of town, and I don't see her as much as I'd like. But if Kim is needed or there is a holiday or special event, the three hours' drive is nothing for her to get here. I have seen Kim come into Louisville for something and get up early the next morning and drive back to go to work.

There is one memory I have to share. One time we went to Kim's house because of the passing of her mother-n-law. Connie called her to see how Dean was doing. Kim said, "He is quiet." Then she told us, "I am trying to take care of things I can do but right now. I am trying to do the wash and realized I don't have any detergent."

When we went to Kim's house the next day, all the sisters and Mom took her a container of Gain. This gave

Kim something to laugh about and relieved tension when she was so worried about Dean. I think we all laughed until some of us had tears in our eyes. I know I did. To me, this is what sister's do–they help one another.

Kim worked at a college and helped a lot of students achieve what they were studying. One of Kim's gifts was empowering girls. Kim started a space camp along with Michelle and Morehead State University, Space and Science Center and AAUW. It was called SpaceTrek. The theme of SpaceTrek is: "Empower young women in an environment with female role models where they will be motivated and exposed to space science and engineering". One day, Kim asked, "Darlene would you like to help me with SpaceTrek?" I replied yes.

My job at SpaceTrek was being a dorm mom and I also took pictures throughout the week. I was there to help with SpaceTrek, but Kim was empowering me, too. I was included in a discussion with Dr. Ben Malphrus, the director of the Space Science Center, Jennifer Carter, a physics and astronomy teacher from Rowan County, Bob Kroll a Space System Engineer, Michele McNeil, the Program Coordinator, and Kim Boggs, the Camp Coordinator.

I said I was included in the discussion. I wasn't really there to discuss anything. But I was honored that they let me be a part of the discussion even though I didn't add to the conversation. Kim was empowering me by letting me know that I was important enough to be included in conversations with brilliant people.

Kim told me more than once, "Darlene you are always thanking us for helping you, but can't you see you are helping us." I guess it is very hard for me to see that I am helping the family.

Tonya is the sister who asks questions, both political and typical. Tonya has no problem asking who, what, why and how questions. In no way is she rude by asking. She just has a way about her, a gift for getting answers.

I wished sometimes I could have each one of their gifts. However, then I wouldn't be who I am. All three sisters have made a huge difference in my life.

Mom and Dad are wonderful and I am extremely honored that they accepted me as one of their daughters.

I loved going camping with them. Dad would start the fire in the mornings and Mom and I would sit by the fire and talk about simple things. Dad taught me, "The more you learn, the more you earn," and, "When you go somewhere, you leave it better than it was when you got there."

Being a part of this amazing family, I began to learn how to be independent, how to survive without a man in my life, and that no matter how much I wanted a man in my life, a man didn't make life easier. Since I been a part of the family I was able to experience some firsts. I went to Las Vegas; I went on a cruise; I went on camping trips that included many families. It amazed me how they planned the trip and everyone got along. The first camping trip, I was sitting in a huge circle with family and was in awe how everyone took turns talking and sharing experiences. I also learned new camping traditions such as how to make fried pies using a pie iron and how to bake biscuits on the Coleman stove.

My new family reminded me to continue relying on God for everything. They helped me with finances and countless other things I should have known naturally, or should have been taught when I was young but wasn't. It was as though my adoptive family helped the butterfly to come out of her cocoon. They gave me the wings I needed to fly. They set me free.

CHAPTER 13

College

One of the most important things one of my new sisters did was to encourage me to go to college. Tonya asked me one day, "Have you ever thought about going to college?" "No!" I said with a little bit of an attitude.

"I am not smart enough to go to college."

Although I was a pre-school teacher, I didn't think the short-term training I had completed to teach at this level qualified me as "smart enough" to go to college.

When Tonya talked to me about college, I thought there was no way I could do it. I had felt like a failure in high school when I struggled and got a "C." I never wanted to experience that feeling of failure again. One of the things I was soon to learn about my new family was how they don't quit. Tonya kept on me. She kept talking about college and talking about college. You see, they were taught growing up that you could do and be anything you set your mind to. I didn't have this in me...yet.

One day, I finally decided I should just go and meet with the man Tonya has been encouraging me to meet. I was a little curious to hear what he had to say, but mainly I just wanted Tonya off my back. By encouraging me, Tonya opened the door to education. I just had to make the choice to walk through it.

I made the choice to start my education but on the first night of classes, I began to doubt myself after hearing the course requirements. I began using negative self-talk by telling myself I was not smart enough to go to college. Luckily, I had a great teacher, Ms. Yolanda, who listened and nurtured me at the beginning. I told her, "I can hardly speak English, let alone write it." Ms. Yolanda encouraged me to write like I thought I should and she assured me she was there to teach me if I was willing to learn. I must say that God put this caring teacher in my life because I needed someone who loved teaching and really cared about students.

The cohort group I started meeting with was amazing. They were people from all over and they treated me with respect. They were so nice and friendly. As a result of a caring teacher and support from this group, I earned an "A" in my first class. I was so happy! I remember calling Tonya to tell her about my grade. I even called my mom and dad and told them about my accomplishment. Well, actually, I told just about everyone. That first "A" felt so good! It gave me power I had not realized I had. I now knew I could achieve anything if I set my mind to it, and I was ready to learn and earn more "A's."

When my second class started, the teacher asked us why we were continuing our education. I answered the teacher:

"Because I want to build up my self-esteem."

This came as a surprise to Mr. Brown and he asked a few questions. One of them was, "So you don't want to learn?"

"Oh yes, sir, I want to learn, and I will. However, I need to work on my self-esteem. Being in college and obtaining knowledge gives me power. This power then raises my self-esteem."

Mr. Brown smiled at me then said to the class:

"Then let us not disappoint Darlene. Let's help her obtain power."

My favorite class was a business class. The teacher, Mr. Ryan, taught me a great deal. He also gave me something to think about. Mr. Ryan asked us if we had ever thought about asking the company we worked for if there was something we could do for them to make their job easier. So with this question in mind, I talked to my principal, Dr. Young.

"Is there anything I could do to make your job easier, besides just showing up?"

"I would appreciate anything you wanted to do for the children and for Watson Lane Elementary."

That made my job so much easier because I knew I was exactly where I needed to be and to serve.

Due to my sudden change in attitude, I was questioned by people I worked with. I was even accused of brown-nosing. My response to these people was:

> "Just because I say I am here to serve, does not mean I am a servant to all."

I have learned how much of myself to give.

Looking back, some people in my business class thought I was just crazy at first. However, over the course of the next year, they got to know me and we became friends. I have met some great friends that I still have in my life today. Plus, there were a few of them continuing the bachelors program with me.

I won't share details about every class, but I do want to share a paper I was proud of. It was entitled *My Cohort* and was dated July 20, 2009:

> *I need to say that when I started going to college I didn't know what "cohort" was. So I had to look it up in the dictionary. It means a group of people. When I looked, I wondered why they didn't just say "class." It means the same. However, over the years I got to know that this cohort is more than just a class. It is group of people that God has put in my life for a reason. Some of the people in the class have made a big impact on my life for the better. Others have been a thorn in my side. Let me share a few highlights and a few, well, let's just say not-in-agreement with one another.*

When I first started college, I didn't think I was smart enough to go and I was really scared to death. However, with the encouragement of my family, I started late in life. When I walked in the first time, I was scared to death and I was amazed at how these strangers accepted me and let me talk and even listened to me. The men in the class were positive role models for me when I had not had many in my past. The first class started a process that I call me coming out of a cocoon and becoming a butterfly.

With crisis in my life, the cohort was there praying for me and giving me the support I needed to keep me going. It was a positive environment and when I came to class, my mood changed because I was there where I felt wanted, needed, and valued as an individual.

Sure, with the class being big and having a lot of women, there are going to be different opinions. Sometimes we were not on the same page or, I felt, were not even in the same book. However, no matter what, when the class was over, we all were still supporting one another to be the best that each of us could be.

It has been an honor to be in this cohort and I can't wait until the next class to see what we can learn.

On the side of my paper next to where I wrote that I started college late in my life, the professor wrote, "At least you started!" Those four words were powerful—so powerful—to a single mom.

Some of the classes I had to take were interesting and some were boring. I must say a couple of them were downright hard, especially the math classes. I had to rely on others to get me through those classes. At no time did others do the work. Tonya and Charissa who helped were harder on me than the real teacher. They were the greatest teachers because they cared about me and they should receive an "A" for putting up with my whining.

Each class empowered me a little more, improved my writing skills and gave me knowledge beyond words. Encouraging words written on my papers by my professors gave me confidence and empowered me even more. Those little words have made me realize what others already knew:

I was and am capable of going to college. I am important in the lives of many people. I was and I am somebody!

CHAPTER 14

Brain Tumor

My headaches started to come more frequently and the pain was getting worse. I thought I was having headaches because of all the stress I was going through. Another reason for the headaches could be hereditary because my father had them all of his life. Those, however, were not the only two reasons. I didn't know there would be a worst-case scenario.

After I got married to Clint, I had more headaches. I thought it might be because of stress. One day I had a headache so bad that Clint even had to help me put on my shoes to go to the ER.

The diagnosis was always, "It's a migraine." I would get a shot and then I would sleep all of the next day. The headaches continued for years. Sometimes I would have a bad headache and the best way to describe it would be as if Freon was going through the veins in my head. They felt so cold.

One day, after having much stress in my life and getting ready to divorce Johnny, I passed out while I was working in my classroom. I don't really know what happened. Afterwards, I learned what happened from Michelle, Ms. Pat and Ms. Windy. I had been sitting on the floor reading to the children when I just fell over. Ms. Windy called for help and the children were taken to Ms. Michelle's class. The ambulance was called, and I was taken to the hospital. Tests showed that I had a brain tumor and I had also had a TIA mini-stroke at some point. What was odd about the whole thing is that my soon- to-be ex-husband, Johnny, couldn't get a divorce fast enough! He was worried about the amount of my medical bills.

I was told that this was the best kind of brain tumor to have because they are usually 99% non-cancerous. However, the tumor started growing faster than the doctor liked and I needed to go get a second opinion. After I got it, the doctor agreed with Dr. Gregory Nazar that I should have an operation. What was different between both doctors was Dr. Nazar said I would be off 6 weeks and the other doctor said I would be out 6 months. I told my sister-in-law Diane, who had gone with me to my appointment, that I needed to go back to see Dr. Nazar because he said I would be off work for six weeks. I only had five weeks of sick days saved up.

The date was set so that the operation would take place on a Saturday since it was the least busy day. I wasn't scared at all. What I worried about were Renae and Mikey. I didn't want to leave them.

While I was in surgery, Renae and Mikey, some members of my real family—Terry and Jamie, members of my adoptive family—Connie, Tonya, Vic and Diane, Mom and Dad, Raquel and Brian and many more, and my church family—Cindy and Doug, Gary and Connie—were all in the waiting room. There were so many praying for me, and I was at peace with it. I told Dr. Nazar that I only had five weeks of paid time off. I desperately wanted him to make it so I could go back to work after that time. He just smiled at me.

What worried me more than anything was waking up from the surgery and someone seeing me without my dentures. I know that might have been silly to worry about, but I hate having a partial. So Renae promised me that she would be the first one to come back to the recovery room. She kept her word.

Dr. Nazar went out to the waiting room and told everyone that the surgery went well. Then my children came back, but I really don't remember who else came to see me. I needed rest and they were just waiting for me to be moved to another room.

Well, after a little while I told the recovery nurse that I couldn't feel my left side. She said she would be right back because she was going to call the doctor. I asked her to please call my family first so they could start praying, and she did as I asked. When the nurse called Mikey, he was at Connie's house and they were on their way back. He made a comment that he was scared.

Dr. Nazar came and told me that these things were normal and they would take a CT scan to see what was going on. The scan showed that my brain was swelling. Dr. Nazar told me that he would give me some medicine.

In the recovery room, the nurse stayed and talked to me after I had been given the medicine. In no time, the feeling started coming back to my left side. The two of us were the only ones on the recovery floor. She was dancing in the aisle. We were praising God for His protection. She said that she had never seen the outcome of prayer like that before. I was moved to ICU because they wanted to watch me closely. The only thing about this is that I couldn't have a lot of visitors. I needed people around me. I needed to see my family, too. However, I needed to rest so I could start to heal. But I also needed to stay positive. I asked the nurse:

"Is there any way I can have visitors?"

"If you don't get overwhelmed with a lot of visitors then I will see what I can do."

"Thanks."

Everything worked out fine. I stayed in ICU until the night before I went home. This was because there was no room anywhere else, so they just kept me there. I was able to move to a regular room the night before I went home. I think this only happened because it wouldn't look good sending a patient home from ICU after a brain surgery.

I had to trust God that He would take care of my family and me. I was so ready to leave the hospital and go home. I didn't really go home, though. I went to my adoptive family's house since I couldn't be left alone after just having had brain surgery. It happened to be the week that Renae and Mikey were at their father's house. I needed to go somewhere, so my Mom and Dad said I could come to their house. I was blessed to have an adopted family. I call Joyce and Glenn my "Mom and Dad." I did that to make my family and friends less confused when I talked about my family and adoptive family.

I always said I will write a book one day, but there are too many characters. I also said I would have to have a list of the people and who they are to keep everyone straight. I still think that is a great idea.

Mom and Dad picked me up from the hospital, and Mom thought I should go see my mother so we stopped on the way home. My mother seemed happy to see me. I introduced Joyce and Glenn and told my mother I was going to their house to stay for a few days. Joyce told my mother that they were treating me as one of the family and that they needed to get me home. My mother said, "Thanks for taking care of Darlene." Nothing else.

As I got in the vehicle, I was relieved that my mother didn't make a scene. I knew it was the right thing to do to stop to see my mother and show her I was doing okay. I wished my mother would have said one thing—that she loved me. Those three words would have made a huge difference in my life.

By the time we got home, I was exhausted. My Dad made a bed where I could sleep upstairs so I could be close to my parents. When I laid down on the bed, I thought it was the softest bed I had ever lain on. It didn't take me long to get to sleep. The care that was given to me is indescribable. The love that I felt was awesome. My mom even tucked me in at night. That was the first time I had ever been tucked in.

"Goodnight, don't let the bed bugs bite."

I think every child should have the privilege of being tucked in at night.

I stayed with Mom and Dad for a couple of days, then went back home. Renae and Mikey were coming back home and I wanted to be there. When I returned home, I was happy to be there. I received so many cards in the mail. One day my Sunday school class even sent me flowers.

When Renae and Mikey came in, I was so happy! They took very good care of me. When they had to go back to school on Monday, I cried because I wanted so badly to go back to work and get on with my life.

I had a journal in the waiting room of the hospital entitled *Faith, Family and Friends*. Inside the front cover, I had written this:

To my Family and Friends,

I want to thank you for being here for Renae and Mikey and I.

This book is for you to write encouraging words to me to read later on. If you don't write something, that is okay. But you will still need to sign that you were here.

Thanks again for all the cards, prayers and most of all LOVE.

Darlene

When my kids left for school, I thought this was a great time to read the book I had asked everyone to sign and write in. There were forty-one entries altogether. Each and every one of them was special. I read:

Well, mom here I am in the waiting room at the hospital and within 2 hours you will be out of the operating room. Mikey

Mom, you will be getting to see "my beautiful face" everyday so get prepared! Just kidding anyway, I love you and hope that you recover fast and easy.   *Love, Renae*

Darlene,

You are loved by your friends and family, but most importantly by your Heavenly Father. May you bask in His Glory as you recover and continue to serve Him. Thank you for allowing me to have a part in your family. It's an honor to know you, Mikey and Renae.

Brad Burns

Darlene

> *We are here waiting and thinking how glad to know you and have you and your children as part of our family. Remember our Bible verse. See you soon.   Joyce*

Darlene,

My prayers and thoughts are with you.

Get Well Soon. 28 days 'til the Next Trip!

> *Love Tonya*

Sis,

From reading these from your friends at the waiting room, I know you have wonderful Christian friends, Sis, I have prayed for you and claim thru Christ that you will be fine. I pray that your recovery will be short. You are my favorite sister, and I want you to know that I love ya very much, I'm glad we stay in touch as brother and sister, Remember I love ya,

    Your brother, Terry

Darlene,
Are you happy?
I signed it!
    Love Jamie

Hey Brat!

    Guess What! Once again you are center of attention. Everyone here is here because they care about you and hope you come out soon. I hope you get well soon. You will be missed at work. You know if you need anything all you have to do is call me.

    Love ya!
    Your friend, Michelle

Darlene,

Well, I'd say this little problem of yours beats my "little problem," this time. But don't keep trying to out-do me, I'll win!

I can't really begin to tell you that amount you mean to me. Your faith, joy, and huge smile, always blows me away! I know you always say that you are blessed because you are "in the family" with us, but, I'm beyond blessed to have you in my life. You're awesome!

I've assembled quite the team that is praying for you, and I won't stop 'til we're making blankets together again!

I LOVE YOU, ROCK

Hi Darlene, Get Well Soon!   Zachary Bruner

Darlene,

It was great to hear from you Friday night. What is great about our relationship is we can go months without talking to each other but our friendship never waivers...I feel just as close today as I ever had. You should always know if you need me call me. I love you always,

Sheila

*Wow! I feel so much since I seen you. You look
great, you miracle girl! God knew I needed my
sister. I love you so much!*   *Charissa*

Some just signed their name and I was blown away by
how many were there for me:

*Connie and Doug; The Great Terry; Janet; Get
Well Soon – Brian and Rock; Patricia and
Grandma Jones; Ross was here; Kevin and kids.*

The pages in the book encouraged me then when I
was sitting on the floor and feeling sorry for myself
because I couldn't go to work. I heard, "You just had a
brain operation, be still and know I am God."

After I heard that, I thought: *The pain pills must be
really working or I am losing my mind.* I knew in my
heart what I heard was from God. So from then on, I didn't
cry because I couldn't go to work. I took the time to rest,
heal and talk to God.

One day when I was bored and I just had to do
something I thought I would just pick up a little because I
never knew if someone would stop by. As I was doing that
I found an email in which Renae was keeping Cindy
updated on me. The email had been posted on a forum for
Valley View:

"Thank you, Cindy, for posting the update! Well,
there is more to update now!! Saturday night

mom's left side went numb, and they did a CAT scan and found that her brain was swelling. They gave her medicine to make it stop swelling.

Yesterday the nurses got mom to sit up in a chair to eat her dinner and I got the report that she did it very well. She wants to come home on Tuesday and go back to work in five weeks but we all think that she is rushing it a bit.

The only thing I am concerned about after we get her home is that the pain medication will not take care of the pain. But thank you all for your prayers and I will try to keep you updated.

Cindy and Doug, God bless you two. I don't think that you two and Brad know how much you all impacted me when you came. I expected everyone else to come but when I saw you all, my thought was that you really care about us.

THANK YOU SOOOO MUCH!!!   Renae."

My heart was full of pride for the way Renae kept everyone updated on me. I also realized that she was worried and scared for me and our family. I prayed for Renae as I was sitting on the side of her bed. I prayed that she would feel my love even when I am not around her for a few days. I didn't know how things were going to work out, but I know that Proverbs 3: 5-6 says, "(5) Trust in the Lord with all your heart and lean not on your own understanding; (6) in all your ways acknowledge him, and he will make your path straight" (Prv. 3:5-6 NIV).

Everyone told me to enjoy this time off. However, I always felt better when I was doing something. I also knew that if I sat around and did nothing, I would get depressed. So, each day I did a little bit more and made sure I rested. A few days after being home, I used a cane that someone gave me and went outside. I even walked down the street. I would say that I walked a good block. I took my time walking back then went to sit on the couch. I thought to myself that I wouldn't tell anyone about what I had just done because they would say I was rushing things. They would probably be right.

The time came for me to get my stitches out. A friend from church, Sam, came to pick me up. He was my angel. He prayed for me when I first found out that I had a tumor. He also sent cards and told me that no matter what, God loves me. Before I had the operation, Sam took me to dinner and we talked about my fears. He had health issues and been through some tough times. Sam gave me a Bible verse on a piece of paper after I shared how scared I was in our Sunday school class. It was: Be joyful in hope, patient in affliction, faithful in prayer" (Rom. 12:12 NIV). When he offered to take me to the doctor, I thought Sam would be the perfect person to take me.

Dr. Nazar was happy that I was doing well. He took the stitches out and said everything was great. I asked him:

"When can I go back to work?"

"Whenever you feel like you can."

"Then can I go back on Monday?"

He said yes! Oh, my goodness! What a miracle!

When Sam and I left there, it was a great feeling. God had worked a miracle. Sure, I would have to go back for a check-up, however the doctor was amazed at how well I was doing. I told him it was because people were praying for me. He said, "Well, you must have had a whole lot of people praying for you."

Sam and I knew that our God was a big God. After we left the doctor, we went to Bob Evans even though I looked like crap. However, Sam didn't care. My hair was a mess because I hadn't been able to wash it, which I was looking forward to doing. When Sam dropped me off at the house, I was so happy. I gave Sam a Willow Tree angel, and he told me he was blessed to have me as a friend.

When Sam left, I started burning up the telephone line. I called Connie and told her the great news. Then I called the rest of my family. There was one more phone call that I wanted to make and it was to my principal, Dr. Young. I told her that I had just come back from the doctor and had been released to go back to work. She seemed very happy for me. I told her that I would see her on Monday. She asked, if I had a note to return. I know that she was just protecting me. I told her yes.

The one sad thing about this, to me, was how some people said I should stay off work as long as I could. My reply to that was, "How can I do that when God gave me a miracle?" I could not mess with this blessing and I would not be quiet about what God had done in my life. I wrote this email to my pastor:

> *Pastor Kevin:*
> *I know you are busy but I need to thank you for the gift card that you sent me. That was very thoughtful of you.*
> *I wrote this for the Kingdom Seekers, really it applies to all Valley Viewers.*
> *To thank everyone for the love that I felt and still am feeling.*

> *Hey Valley Viewers*
> *I have something to say,*
> *Listen closely.*
> *So you can hear,*
> *Without delay.*
> *Last Saturday,*
> *Even before noon.*
> *I could feel the love that was in my room.*
> *Even after everyone was gone away*
> *There was never a shortage of prayers,*
> *coming my way.*
> *Even though I was*
> *scared to death.*
> *God was with me*
> *for my every breath.*
> *God gets all the glory,*

right from the start.
Everyone here gets a thank you,
from my heart.
Thanks for your time,
Darlene

I know without a doubt that I could not have gotten through the storm without the love and support from my family, friends and our church.

I remember going to the altar and getting on my knees and giving God praise for seeing me through. Then there was a hand on my back. I looked over and there was Mikey. And then there was another hand. I looked to the other side and there was Renae. By the time I finished praying and giving God all the praise, a whole lot of people surrounded us. Like Renae mentioned in the email, it showed me that there were people who really cared about us.

The only thing that could make me rethink going back to work happened. One day, as I was sitting on the floor playing a game, a little girl didn't like how the game was being played so she grabbed my hair right at the incision where it was still tender. She would not let go. Ms. Christina ran across the hall to get Michelle and they had to pry the little girl's hands off me. That day I saw stars and shed tears. From then on, I didn't sit on the floor until I was fully recovered.

Having the brain tumor really changed me. There was food that I liked before the operation, but not after. Then there was food like broccoli that I used to hate, but now I wanted it all the time.

Another thing that was different after the operation was that I didn't remember a lot from the past. It seemed some days I could remember things and others day it was just a blank. Renae would say, "Mom, remember when we did this?" On some days I would just have to say, "No, I don't remember."

Renae told me later on that I was mean before finding out I had a brain tumor. There is really no way to say I was mean because of the brain tumor. However, on some days I wonder if our life would have been different in my marriages if we found out there was a medical reason and it could have been fixed.

I must say that my marriages to Clint and Johnny who I married twice could have failed because of my childhood. However, I will never know. I also know that they both put up with a lot being married to me. I had so much pain from my past and I brought it into the marriages. I hope and pray that one day that they can forgive me.

CHAPTER 15

House Fire

After my brain tumor surgery, it seemed like I could never get warm. I would put extra blankets on my bed and I even wore pajamas to bed. I also got myself an electric heater.

On March 22 when I went to bed, it seemed as though I was cold from the inside out. So when I went to bed, I plugged in my heater and fell asleep. I needed to get up early so I set my alarm. I heard Mikey's alarm go off in my head. I needed to get up but I was tired. I was getting hot so I turned over to turn off the heater. However, what I saw was a small fire so I rolled back over, got out of the bed and ran to Mikey's room. I yelled, "My room is on fire." Mikey ran to my room with me. I asked my seventeen-year-old son what I needed to do and he told me to get him some water. Renae heard us talking and I told her to get water, too.

When I went back into the room, Mikey had taken a towel and was trying to put the fire out by swinging the towel back and forth. I gave him my water. He threw it on the fire but it didn't help. Renae's water wasn't much help because she carried her water in a box. When Mikey and I woke Renae up, she was disoriented and didn't really understand at first what was going on.

The fire kept growing so I told them to get out of the house and call 911. The smoke was getting so thick and I wanted to make sure they were okay. For a split second, I thought about needing my purse. However I didn't know where I had put it. I had to get my children out of the burning house. I walked out of the front door and I just fell to the ground and screamed, "I can't take any more!"

At that time, Mikey ran next door to get our neighbor and Renae was talking to her boyfriend. I asked her to call Connie. Renae called my sister and also called Michelle. Michelle and her two children, Zachary and Camryn, came right over. Michelle said that she smelled smoke but didn't know where it was coming from until Renae called her. Zachary said, "I will never forget this day because today is my birthday."

We stood in the front yard waiting for the fire trucks and firemen to come. Mikey and the neighbor got water hoses and tried to get the fire under control. Renae went back into the house because I told her we needed to move the cars so the fire trucks would have room. However, I didn't think she would go back into a burning house to get them. The keys were hanging by the front door on a key holder and she grabbed the whole thing.

Watching your house go up in flames is awful. In the background, we heard sirens but they seemed so far away. Neighbors were coming out and waiting for the firemen. It was terrible to watch it seemed like hours before they finally arrived.

We soon found out that Mikey got burned when he was trying to put the fire out. The paramedic thought Mikey should go to the hospital to make sure he didn't have smoke inhalation. Connie arrived then and she drove me to the hospital following the ambulance.

I looked down and noticed that I had a housecoat on that wasn't mine and a pair of house shoes that also weren't mine.

Renae called her father and Clint came to the hospital, too. The doctor said Mikey was fine and that he could go home. A fireman from the arson division came to the hospital. He told us it was normal for him to ask questions. He also told us that the fire was contained to one room, my bedroom. We thanked him and he said he would be in touch. When we left the hospital, Mikey rode with his father and Connie took me back to the house.

When Connie and I drove in front of the house, we noticed that the fire trucks were gone and that there was a restoration van there. I walked in and I asked them who they were. They said they had heard about our fire and decided to come over to see if they could help us. That was when Connie spoke up and said, "So you heard about the fire and just decided to come over?" I thought this was a little overwhelming. Connie followed with, "You can leave your card and if Darlene decides to use you, she will be in touch."

Although the fireman had told me the fire was contained in one room, he didn't prepare me for what I walked into. My bedroom was gone. Everything! The firemen had broken my windows and everything had been taken out. There was nothing left. There was smoke all through the house. The mini blinds were all melted, and the front window was broken. I just couldn't believe it. It was all ruined!

Gary from our church came over and boarded it up and told me I couldn't stay there. I found my purse that was sitting right by the front door. The purse was a little bit burned on the top, but everything in it was okay. Leaving my home was very hard. I wanted to stay to fix it, clean it up and make it better, but I didn't have the skills to do that. I would have to ask for help.

Connie drove me to Wal-Mart, because I had to get myself some clothes. I looked down as we were walking into the store and I reminded Connie that she had told me I could never go to the store in my pajamas.

"I will make this a onetime exception."

We laughed and went in the store. I think I was laughing to keep from crying.

We went to Connie's house where I took a shower. It was really sad for me because now all I owned fit into two Wal-Mart bags.

Later that night, I checked on Renae and Mikey and reassured them that I was all right and that we would get the house fixed. Thank God we had insurance. When I went to bed that night, I thanked God for saving my two children and me.

I didn't sleep well that night. I kept on dreaming about the fire. I woke up sweating, because I was dreaming that Renae couldn't get out. Then I realized I was in a different place and that I was just dreaming.

I got up and went to the living room and found Connie was already up. She asked, "How did you sleep?" I replied, "Not very good." Connie took me back to my house. I wanted to be there when the insurance man came. Plus, I wanted to walk through the house again.

I called work again and told them I couldn't come in. They understood and told me if there was anything they could do for me, they would. I thanked them.

The insurance man came and looked at everything. He told me that everything would be okay. He asked me if I had a place to stay. I told him for right now I wanted to be around my family. He gave me his card and told me that he would be handling the claim and to call him if I needed anything. He said he would send over a cleaning crew and they would try to save some of my things. He also said there would be a dumpster here, too. All of my things were lying in the backyard beneath my windows.

The crew of people the insurance called over to my house were quick. I was glad I was there because I told them what could go in the dumpster and what I wanted to try to save. My friend Terry and a couple of guys picked up everything that was under my bedroom window and threw it in the dumpster.

Then another restoration company came and took all the clothes, towels curtains and anything else that could be washed and possibly saved. They even took the dirty laundry. They took it to be cleaned and stored until I got back into the house.

My emotions were all over the place. I would cry, then I would laugh because I didn't want to cry. I would get mad, because I lost things that no one could replace. But then I thought I was really blessed, because no one got seriously hurt.

Michelle came over after work to check on me. She said I could stay with her if I wanted to. Ms. Pat, Dale and their grandson Ray came over, too. I had some amazing co-workers who became my friends.

Connie stopped by to see how I was holding up. She had found a house that I could rent while the house was being fixed. I followed Connie to the house. It was close to our church and not too far from our home in case we needed to run over there for something. It would also allow me to bring Renae and Mikey back home where I wanted and needed them. I think we all needed each other. Plus, it would help out a woman named Eleanor who was trying to sell the house. *God is good all the time. All the time, God is good.*

I called the man from the insurance company about renting the house and getting things I needed so I could get my family back together again. He told me to get a lease together and he would send me a check to buy some things. He suggested that I rent some furniture. However, I didn't want to waste their money. I told him, "I will just buy it, that way you won't have to pay for me to rent furniture and then pay to have it replaced." I think he was surprised by my reply.

I stopped by the insurance place to get a copy of my policy to see what I had, because I really didn't know what kind of coverage I had. The insurance agent told me to look for the silver lining in the fire.

I left there and thought, "Silver lining? There is no silver lining I can see right now." Renae lost her prom dress and her grandmother's jewelry box. Mikey didn't know where the quilt went that was his grandmother's. He hoped it was in the possession of the company that took everything to clean and that it hadn't burned up in the fire. The sentimental things couldn't be replaced.

We moved into the rental house and stayed there until our house was ready for us to move back into. I asked Gary, who boarded up the house when it burned, if he would be my contractor because I didn't know anything about putting a house back together. He agreed. I liked it because Gary went to our church, was in my Sunday school class, and had a son who was Mikey's friend.

Gary gave me advice about the house. He also said he could save me some money if Mikey was willing to tear the bathroom apart. The money we saved in one place, we could add to something else. It was a great idea.

Mikey and I tore the bathroom apart. It had a small closet that wasn't essential, so we took sledge hammers and a pry bar and tore it up. I think at one point I was taking my anger out on the walls.

Just like before, we had people surround us with love and prayers. My family was awesome. Watson Lane Elementary School amazed me with their support.

And my God will meet all your needs according to his glorious riches in Christ Jesus. (Phil. 4:19 NIV)

God did meet all of our needs. Finally, I was able to see the silver lining. It was the day we moved back into our house, a far better house after the fire than it was before. This experience made me not take people for granted. It made me not be caught up in material things. It made me appreciate the family and friends I had in my life.

I also saw Renae and Mikey grow up as young adults. Renae took care of me for a while because, on some days, I didn't know what to do. I have called my son Mikey ever since he was born, however he wanted to be called

Mike now, especially out in public. I told him I will try. But he will always be Mikey to me.

CHAPTER 16

Between God and Me

In my Bible, I keep some index cards. On the index cards, written in red, I have these questions: God, who do I tell? God, what do I do? God, how do I go on? Why? If I am weak, how do I get through whatever I have planned for the day? How do I serve you?

I think I keep this in my Bible as a reminder of how I chose to keep a medical problem between God and me. I know the reasons why I did it, however it doesn't justify the hurt I caused to my family and friends.

Everyone is different in the way they conduct themselves to get through a storm. How they choose to do it should be up to the person. A very special lady named Kathy gave me a quote that I still use today: "Fake it 'til you can make it."

Still to this day no one understands why I did it. However, I made a commitment with God. I would depend on Him for His love, grace and mercy.

My memory took me back in time to when I was eleven and I went to the dentist on the corner of 27th and Portland. I was having pain in my jaw and it hurt really badly. With my mother being on welfare, she could take us to the dentist and doctor for free. My mother went with me because she had to show them her medical card.

The dentist looked at my mouth and noticed I had a few cavities. He also saw that there was something wrong with the enamel on my teeth. He asked if I brushed my teeth every day. I said, "Not every day, it depends if we have toothpaste or not." He told me that I should still rinse out my mouth even if I didn't have toothpaste. He then told the assistant to give me some toothpaste when I left. He told me that the chance of me losing my teeth by the age of 40 was great, because of how my mouth looked. The dentist told my mother that I needed to come back to get the cavities filled. He told her that it was very important for me to see him at least once a year after he took care of the cavities.

I left there feeling sad. I didn't want to lose my teeth. I wanted to keep my real ones. When I got home, I put the toothpaste he gave me in my drawer. I thought about keeping all the toothpaste to myself since he had given it to me, but I felt bad about that. I didn't want my sisters or brothers to have bad teeth, so I took two tubes of toothpaste and put them in the bathroom.

I tried to take care of my teeth from then on. I didn't want Raymond brushing my teeth with Comet and I wanted to keep my teeth until my last days on this earth.

However, that was not going to happen to me. I started having trouble with my teeth when I was living in Evansville, Indiana. I had to have one of my back teeth pulled. They could have done a root canal on it, but I didn't have the money to pay for it.

When I returned to Louisville, I was still having trouble with my teeth. I would go to the dentist and get them fixed when I could. However, I was told my gums were awful. So, I made sure I brushed my teeth and flossed regularly.

One day as I was going to pick up Renae from the daycare, I stopped at the store and bought a bag of chips and a Big Red. While I was eating my chips, I felt something hard. I spit out what was in my mouth into a Kleenex and saw what looked like a piece of my tooth, so I pulled over to the side of the road and looked in the mirror. It was a tooth from the back of my mouth.

From then on, my teeth slowly started to break. In my mind, I could still hear the dentist saying that by the age of 40 I would have false teeth. I still took care of my teeth the best I could for the next ten years. I was thirty years old and was so afraid of what I would look like if I didn't have any teeth at all.

I feared that I would embarrass Johnny, Renae and Mike if I didn't have any teeth. My mother used to whine and carry on about how false teeth felt and how you couldn't eat this or that. My mother sometimes would take her teeth out and leave them in a cup. I thought that was so gross! I decided that if I did get false teeth I would not take my teeth out and put them in a cup.

The day came that I dreaded. It was the day I had the last four of my top teeth pulled. Mr. Tucker took me to the dentist because Johnny had to work. Then he took me to Kroger's to drop off my prescription and then back home. Johnny took care of me that evening and Clarissa had called to check on me.

I went back to the place where I had my partial made to get a full set for my top. I was in shock that I couldn't have them made that day. They said it was too soon. I had to wait at least three weeks. There was no way I could go without my teeth for three weeks. I thought to myself that I had enough sick days to cover the days off.

So I washed my tear-stained face and called my principal, Dr. Young, after I got home hoping she wouldn't hear how upset I was when I talked to her. After I asked to speak to her she came on the line.

"Hi, Darlene how are you feeling?"

"I hate to tell you this, but I need three weeks off from work."

"Are you alright?"

"Yes, I am fine, but I went to get my teeth and they can't do them now. They said it is too early, that I need to heal."

At that moment I started crying and told Dr. Young that I was sorry.

"No reason to be sorry for crying, but I think you will be just fine and you need to come to work."

"But Dr. Young, I have no teeth."

"That will be okay. The children will accept you as you are. Plus, it will be a teachable moment for the children. I will see you Tomorrow."

Then she said goodbye and hung up the phone.

Teachable moment. You've got to be kidding me. There is no way I could go to work. I was not worried about the children because Dr. Young was right, they would accept me. It was the co-workers I was worried about.

I talked to Johnny and he said I should take the sick days that were mine. That night when I went to bed. I prayed to God:

God,
You know how I feel about my teeth and face. How can I go to school with no teeth? Please be with me and help me make the right decision. Amen.

The next morning, I woke up and got ready for work. When I looked in the mirror, I saw the little girl that had her teeth brushed with Comet. One tear went down the side of my face.

In my head there was a faint whisper, "I will be with you." So I went to work, and the children and my co-workers were great. Yes, I did shed some tears. They all told me that I was where I should be and it was better than being at home getting depressed.

After I got my upper plate I looked a little different. I was happy to have teeth. One child told me on the first day with my new teeth, "When you go to bed at night make sure you know where you put them. My granny is always looking for hers." I laughed and said that was great advice, coming from a four-year-old.

It was hard getting used to them. Over time I started getting sores in my mouth, so I would have to go back to the dentist. The dentist sent me to a specialist who informed me that I will have to have some treatments for my mouth. I left there crying and went to the graveyard where my father is buried. I just cried and talked to my father. Then I talked to God. When I left there, I knew what I was going to do. I would go on as if nothing was wrong and depend on God for everything.

In hindsight, I hurt a lot of people including the two people I love more than myself, Renae and Mike. They were always the last to know that I was or am sick. I wanted to protect them.

Renae even said, "Now I know why you made a bucket list and watch the movie *Bucket List* over and over. You thought you were going to die." I did think I was going to die, but there was something worse than dying. It was the reflection in my mirror. I didn't like what I saw in the mirror.

When I get ready for bed after having my bath that I still love to take until this day, I take my teeth out and the reflection I see in the mirror is always the child that had her teeth brushed with Comet. No one can say that the Comet caused all my dental problems. However, it didn't help either.

Sometimes when I am looking at myself in the mirror, I see that pretty girl at seventeen who would stop at the mirror in her mother-in-law's house and say, "Damn I look good." The laughter of others who were listening to me at that time was music to my ears.

I think sometimes that dying would have been easier because I would be healed in heaven. I would have perfect teeth. I would smile so big and not have to worry about my mouth.

"For I know the plans I have for you," declares the Lord, "plans to prosper you and not to harm you, plans to give you hope and a future" (Jer. 29:11 NIV). I clung to that verse on most days because I wanted a future. I wanted to be happy with the face in the mirror. I wanted someone to love me and look past the face to my heart where I had so much love to give.

I knew that I could trust God with anything and everything and also that God put people in my life for reasons: to get through all kinds of storms, good times and bad, sickness and health, to pray for me and my family, to encourage me, and especially to love me.

I learned to stop keeping things from my children, Renae and Mike. I promised them that I would tell them first if anything good or bad was going on with me I learned that I didn't have to keep things to myself anymore like I had done as a child. I've learned that the face in the mirror is the face that God loves, with or without teeth.

CHAPTER 17

Too Good to Be True

After taking the time to find out who Darlene was, I thought it was time to date again. However, I still went about it the wrong way. I trusted what people said and I didn't look for red flags.

I met Kelly at a book store. I was in the Christian book section and he asked me if the book I was looking at was a good book. I said I didn't know yet, as I hadn't read it. We chatted and I ending up giving him my phone number. I was thinking that it was better than meeting a man at a bar or a singles dance.

That night he called me and said that I could email him, so I did and we talked all the time. Kelly was a salesman. He wasn't home much, which was okay with me because at that time I was going through a lot and I didn't need to be tied down to a man.

Kelly was a different kind of man than I had ever dated before. He dressed like a professional all the time. All his clothes matched. He wore a lot of Ralph Lauren. He also smelled oh so good. His language was awesome and I could just sit and talk to him for hours. On our first date, we met at Mimi's Café for lunch. The invitation he left on my machine was in a voice like a southern man from the 1800's. I had to listen to it a few times to understand it; I even let Michelle listen to it.

When I met Kelly at Mimi's, he gave me a big hug. He opened the door for me which was so nice. When we sat down, we just made small talk. I was so nervous. He patted me on the arm and said, "You are safe." I relaxed a little. A song came on over the speaker system. Kelly started singing to me. His voice was so awesome! I was hooked from that moment on.

Kelly sang me a song that I had never heard before and the lyrics were, "I know him by heart." The song was about a woman looking for a man and even though she had never met him or heard him speak, she would know him by heart. I was thinking: *Wow!*

After lunch, Kelly wanted to know if I would like to take a walk or to see where he lived. I said I would like to know where he lived and I felt safe, so we went to his apartment. It was very nice and elegant. I couldn't believe a man had decorated this apartment because it was great. Kelly told me that he used to work as a writer in New York and had been in plays. From his singing abilities, I could see why. We didn't stay there long because Kelly had to head to Tennessee for business and wouldn't be back in town until the following week. He said we would keep in touch. Then he gave me a new work shirt of his and sprayed it with his cologne so I would remember him.

I was going to a Sunday school retreat where I was going to speak for the first time, and I was happy that I had met a man who liked me for me. I picked up Charrisa who was going with me. We have become instant friends the first time we met. Charrisa had been through many things with me and had seen me make mistakes but still loved me. I call her my soul mate. I didn't know that two women could be soul mates and have a love for each other that was non-sexual. However, it is true. I've talked to Charissa about everything and I have even trusted her with things that my ex-husbands didn't know.

We laughed and talked all the way to the conference and Charissa cried as I talked about my life in front of my Sunday school class. This was the speech that I gave. It was great looking into the crowd and seeing Charrisa, as she was one of my biggest supporters.

Hi,

I want to take a few minutes to thank Doug for giving me this opportunity to speak and dance for you. But most of all, I want to thank God.

A few months ago I had to get up in front of a class of only 26 people and I was scared to death. Moreover, I was overweight and I couldn't perform the dance as well as the performance I had seen on the computer. However, these obstacles did not matter. God loves me and He loves the fact that I overcame these obstacles and that I stepped out of my comfort zone for him.

I need to start the journey of taking care of myself as I had promised God. I made a promise to God when I was having my brain operation that if he got me through, I would start taking care of myself. Well, I didn't do it right away. It took me a little time to get started.

I think God has a sense of humor because when I was in a Life of Christ class, I had to get up in front of the class and give my interpretation of Matthew 5-9. Well, I knew I didn't like that area of the Bible because it hits too close to my heart. In the passage, the Bible mentions divorce which I have experienced three times. But the teacher, Mr. Clark, said that since it was my interpretation, I could include what I chose to include. However, I had to at least talk for 12 minutes.

Sure, I know what you are thinking, 12 minutes is not long. I have the reputation of being the "social butterfly." I also know that this was a different experience than talking to someone one-on-one, which I can do very well. In a classroom I had to share with 26 other people. That was very different. Twelve minutes seemed like forever. On a legal pad in front of me I wrote down, "God, I need your help if you want me to do this."

So when I got home, I got on my computer and typed the words "voice of truth." These words had stuck in my head. My computer search resulted in a video of a man dancing to the song *Voice of Truth*. At that moment, I just laughed out loud. There was no way that I could do this dance! However, I heard a voice saying, "Yes you can." So for the next four days, I drove Renae and Mikey crazy by playing this song and video over and over. When I got up and tried to perform the dance, there was no way that I could perform as well as the man because of my weight. It didn't really matter because God loves me anyway and he loves the fact that I am willing to step out of my comfort zones for him.

I later found out that it didn't matter because that night I was dancing for Jesus. However, at that moment, I realized that God was telling me something: I needed to lose weight. That is where I say I started walking with Jesus daily.

It has not been an easy road to lose the weight but every day I put one foot in front of the other and took another step in the right direction. I started watching what I ate. Then I came to like walking and still to this day I love walking. I have also started a walking club at Watson Lane Elementary and am trying to get the children involved in taking care of their bodies.

Now I am here trying to motivate people to get involved in losing weight but it is more than that; I am trying to get them to walk with Jesus daily. In other words, to have a relationship with Jesus. We all put stuff in front of Jesus but no matter what, God is always there. He never leaves us. So it is my mission to get the message out there. To tell people that God loves them no matter what.

Sure I have had some major battles: abused as a child, raped as a teen, bad marriages, attempted rape, a brain tumor, depression, and a house fire. But no matter what I was going through, God was there with me all the time. It is how I learned the difference between a problem and an opportunity. This is in no way my definition, but it is a very good one and it comes from a man who has great wisdom. That man is Doug. He says the difference is: a problem is something you try to work out all by yourself, but an opportunity is where God and you work it out together. It sounded funny at first, but I have to agree with Doug.

No matter what you go through, if you know for a fact that there is a God that will be with you in everything, then you are much more equipped with what you need to get through any situation.

Don't be hard-headed like me. Think smarter, not harder. Work with God, not against Him.

So take that leap of faith and start walking with Jesus. You can make your life happier and even find out, if you put your feet where your mouth is, then you might even lose the weight.

The last thing is that I went searching for answers everywhere. I would ask everyone their opinion. I came to realize that humans are not the ones I need to be listening to. Sure there are great role models. But the one I need to listen to is God. He is the Voice of Truth.

I was very surprised by their reactions. What surprised me the most is when they gave me a standing ovation. I started crying. I am so loved by many people.

When we drove home the next day, I spoke to Charrisa about Kelly and she was happy for me. I told her it was too good to be true and that it wouldn't last because Kelly was way out of my league. Of course, Charissa got on me about that statement. However, I get these feelings and most of the time they are right. This time I decided that I would date Kelly if he wanted to. No matter how long it lasted, I would enjoy the ride.

When Kelly was in town, I would go to his side of town and we would go out to eat and spend time just talking and getting to know each other. I was amazed that he wanted to be around me.

He had a way that would charm anyone and I fell for it hook, line and sinker. Though I knew that it was wrong, I did what my flesh was telling me to do. I know now that I was looking for love in all the wrong places. One night Kelly asked me if things didn't work out between us would I still love him and would I still be his friend. When I was driving home, I thought how odd of a question that was.

I told Kelly everything just as I told my girlfriend Charrisa. I was in love with him no matter how long we would be together. With me telling Charrisa everything we did and what we talked about, she thought the same thing that I did. That Kelly was a man to show me how to be loved the right way.

At this time in my life, I had major health issues and I still liked that I didn't have to worry about pleasing a boyfriend. However, there were times that we would make a date and Kelly couldn't make it. He said dating a salesman was hard, so I tried to understand.

The hardest times were when I would make plans with my adoptive family and he would not show up. I would make excuses for him. Doug told me what he thought about Kelly:

"Darlene he might have a girlfriend in every town."

I said that would be fine because when he was here, he was spending time with me. I just didn't believe that Kelly would be that type. He was a Christian man and he prayed for me. When I was having a bad time, Kelly would pray over the phone and he would sing to me.

When I went on a cruise with my family, Kelly and I kept in touch. He couldn't wait until I got back. However, when I got back, he was gone. He was in Tennessee. It was

Thanksgiving time and I was still the one who didn't have a date. Kelly made it up to me when he got back, though. He treated me like a queen.

Christmas was coming and I was planning to go to Ashland to see a David Phelps concert. I asked Kelly if he wanted to go, too. He couldn't because he was leaving for Tennessee to spend a couple of weeks with his sister Sharon. It had been a year since their sister had passed away. He asked if we could celebrate when he got back. I thought that would be great, so I didn't buy him gifts at that time. I asked him then if he would go to a Christmas party with me. It was my life group Sunday school class and I would be honored if he would escort me. He agreed that he would.

That night I was so nervous because he was going to meet my church family and my children. Charrisa came over early to help me get ready and Kelly even called. I froze because I thought he was calling to say that he couldn't come. However, that was not the case. He was coming. His GPS was telling him to go one way and he thought it was wrong. It was right; it was just taking him a longer way.

Charrisa and I were having a good time laughing and getting me ready. I even put on my pantyhose in the car as she was driving to the church.

Kelly did make it. He entered through a different door. I was so happy to see him! Everyone thought Kelly was wonderful and, yes, he even smelled good, too. I told a couple of friends that it wouldn't last, but I was having fun. Everyone got on me when I said that, however deep inside I knew there was no way this man could love me. After the party, Kelly took me home and, fortunately, I had made sure the house was clean. I even cleaned my bedroom. However, there was no way he was staying overnight there. I had children in the house. When we pulled in my driveway I said:

"Kelly you can't stay the night, I have children here."

"Oh Darlene, I am not staying. I have a meeting in Tennessee and I thought I would just drive there from here."

The air went out of me. I put on a face and acted like it was okay. Kelly met my son Mike at church because he was working there and now he was going to meet my daughter. Renae liked him right away. I asked him if he wanted a tour of my house. Renae said, "Yeah, give him a tour of the bedroom that you never use." The way it came out was not what she meant. I didn't sleep in my bedroom.

When Kelly went into my bedroom, he asked me why I didn't sleep there. I said it is nice but it is lonely and I sleep better on the couch, especially when the children aren't home. He lay down on the bed and said, "Darlene, this is a nice bed. Promise me that you will sleep here."

So I made the promise to him that I would start sleeping in my bed. When Kelly left, I was sad because I was hoping we could watch a movie or play some music or something. I just wanted to spend more time with him.

The next time I saw Kelly, it was getting closer to the time when he would be leaving for Tennessee. When I arrived at his apartment, he greeted me like always with a smile and a kiss. By the look of the papers on the table, he had been working. However, it wasn't for work. He was working on a poem for me. It was called *The Christmas Star*.

The Christmas Star

Or

The Amazing Ms. Darlene

It wasn't that long ago she appeared on the scene
And in a quick online "hello", said "Hi, Mr. Bean"
Curious I ventured inside her domain
And soon we were smiling and I
Learned of her name.

Nowabarlow she proclaimed to all of the world
What does that mean? So I gave it a whirl...
"It's about my new life, and the life I now live,
The old me is gone now and I'm learning to give"

And give she does do with her blankets and smile
And occasionally she even does rest for a while.
Her gifts bring us warmth and so does her presence,
If you just take the time to know her
You'll see that's her essence.

Some of her days go better than others
But she never stops being a friend and a mother.

She believes in her God and worships each day
By giving of herself in the most selfless way.

She struggles within and reaches out seldom
And as our prayers go with her
It's obvious, she felt them...
She lives her life real...not a Monroe or a Harlow
That's the joy we do see, that she's Nowabarlow...
So go on forever, you princess and friend
And know that God's with you
And that never ends...
Thank you for being...just who you are
And for all of us Nowa...you're Our Christmas Star!

Merry Christmas my beautiful and cherished friend!

I cried. I'd never had someone write a poem about me. It was beautiful and I was so shocked. Not only did Kelly write a poem, but he had gifts, too. He wanted to give me the gifts because he felt bad about leaving me during the holidays. I didn't want the gifts because I hadn't purchased gifts for him. I wanted to wait until he got back. However, he insisted that I take the gifts. They were not wrapped. He explained that they weren't wrapped because he was rushing around to get everything finished up around the house, and after spending some time with me, he was going to drive to Tennessee.

Kelly gave me a sweater, perfume and the movie *August Rush*. I was smiling inside and out. We left the apartment to go get something to eat. We decided on Smokey Bones. I could've just about gone anywhere to eat with him, because I simply loved being around him.

As we were waiting for our food, I told Kelly that I was going to miss him. He said, "I know and I am sorry that I have to leave our first Christmas. However, I made these plans before I met you and I really do need to go and visit my sister." He promised that he would call me on Christmas, and I asked him if he would call me on one other day. He took out his blackberry and added me to his agenda.

"See...I will call you on December 28th."

Kelly and I went back to his apartment and talked for a little bit then I told him I had to get something out of my car and would be right back. As I was walking out to get the surprise out of my car, my gut instinct was telling me something was not right.

When I got to Kelly's door, I had to ring the doorbell because my hands were full. When Kelly opened the door, his face showed amazement. I was walking in carrying blankets.

"What is this?"

"Remember when I asked you about your family and what they liked and you told me? I made blankets for your children and grandchildren based on the answers you gave me. Plus, I made one for your sister."

"I can't believe you did this for all my family! I had no idea you were going to make blankets for my whole family. How much did this cost? I know, I will write you a check, because there is no way I can take the blankets without paying for them."

"Kelly, there is no need for you to pay me for the blankets. They are a gift for you to give to your family."

"I understand, Darlene, but I must write you a check."

When I looked at the check, he had written it for one hundred dollars. I said, "Thank you," but I really wanted to laugh out loud because he had no idea how much one blanket cost to make. I guess the saying is true...it is the thought that counts.

I was so sad when I left the apartment that night. I really wanted this Christmas to be different then the past few ones. I wanted a man to share the holidays with. Tears and driving just don't mix, but I cried while driving home.

I worked a few more days and then was off for Christmas break. I was going to Ashland, Kentucky, to stay with my sister Kim, and we had plans to attend a David Phelps Christmas concert. As I drove, I thought about how nice it was to have a boyfriend, even though he was gone all the time. I didn't want winter break to go by too fast, but I did want Kelly to be back in Louisville.

Christmas was bittersweet because everyone had someone. I was able to spend a little time with Renae and Mike, then they had to go to their father's. They had a life of their own. After they left on Christmas day, I just had a meltdown.

I was missing Kelly like crazy, especially when I was home alone and the house was so quiet. I sent Kelly a note telling him it had been the longest two weeks of my life and that I couldn't wait until he got back.

The next morning, I was getting ready for work and my cell phone went off. It was Kelly's ring tone, a song by Coldplay, and I rushed to pick it up because I knew I would be talking to the most amazing man. However, when I heard his voice, I knew something was wrong.

Kelly said, "Nowa, I haven't been completely honest with you." I was thinking in my head: *Please don't be married, and please don't be married.*

"The truth is, I have a fiancé who lives in Ohio, and she retrieved the message that you sent me while I was taking a shower."

"So, Kelly, you have a finance' and you're just now telling me about it?"

"Yes, I am sorry. I am worried that she might call you and I need you to tell her that we met because of my friend, Brady, and that I was helping you out, because I knew what it was like having someone sick since my son Dawson was sick, too."

"Let me get this straight. You want me to lie for you!?!"

"Please, Nowa, I need you to do this. I could lose a lot if you don't cover for me. "Sorry Kelly, I have to think about it. Plus, I am crushed because I thought you loved me. You said you adored me. I just don't know what I did for you to treat me like this."

"I still want you in my life, Nowa!"

With that, I hung up and laid on the floor and just cried. I even screamed. I couldn't believe that someone could hurt another person so badly.

I didn't go to work that day. I stayed in bed and cried. Renae came home and I told her I was sick. I called Charissa and within an hour she was at my house. She came in my room and crawled in my bed and we both cried. She told me that she, too, had been fooled.

Going through that week was so hard. I had to tell Renae and Mike what had happened with Kelly. I told them what was happening before telling anyone else because they didn't like being the last ones to know when I was sick or upset.

After a few days, I knew life had to go on even when I didn't understand why it seemed like I was the one who was always getting hurt. Sometimes my life seemed like it wasn't worth living because I kept on making the same mistakes when it came to men. I sat down and wrote Kelly a note about how I felt about his betrayal:

Kelly,

Today didn't start out like I thought it would. When I heard your ringtone going off on my phone, my heart skipped a beat because you make me smile. You were calling me, and I raced to the phone to hear the voice of the most amazing man. However, just hearing your voice, I could tell something was wrong. I tried to be brave on the phone. I tried not to cry.

What I said on the phone is the truth! I will not regret loving you. I will not regret meeting you. After reading the book Boundaries, I have learned a lot; maybe you need to read it again, especially page 230. I wished I had read the book before I met you because I might have handled things differently. However, I do feel that one of the reasons you crossed my path was to give me the book.

I knew when you came back that we needed to talk. I had a gut feeling that something just wasn't right. According to the book, "because of these fears, we try to have secret boundaries. We withdraw passively and quietly, instead of communicating an honest no to someone we love. We secretly resent instead of telling someone that we are angry about how they have hurt us. Often we will privately endure the pain of someone's irresponsibility instead of telling them how their behavior affects us." This is on page 101.

When you didn't call on Christmas, I thought that was odd. I had butterflies in my stomach; a feeling that something was wrong. While we were at Smokey Bones, I asked if you would call me on December 28. That day was very important to me, and at that time you added it to your Blackberry. You made a comment about it, though I can't remember the exact words. I took it to mean you would call me. I had to change the plans for December 28 to December 27 because Renae was sick. So that day was hell, pure hell; I slept for 16 hours, but the next day I knew I would be feeling better because you were calling me.

I am reminded of the new song by David Phelps, Mine. It is so true when it says, "I fall apart and just a word from you somehow seems to fix whatever's wrong." To me, just a word from you made me smile, made me feel good, made me feel loved. But that call never came. My gut was telling me, "This is a RED FLAG!" Something is not right, because if you loved me like you said you did, you wouldn't forget days as important as Christmas and the one day I asked you to call. I just knew I had to talk to you about this, because I wanted to understand how you could forget me, the person who you said time and time again that you loved.

To me, since I do love you, I know without a doubt that I would not have forgotten you. I have not stopped thinking about you since you left. I have been telling everyone how wonderful you are, that you're a family man, and that you were with your sister since this was the year after your younger sister passing. That made you a most amazing man.

The movie that you gave me to watch, I have watched every day because you gave it to me. It also has music in it which seems to make me smile. It was like I was watching you because when "August Rush" was conducting the symphony orchestra, it reminded me of you doing it at your apartment when you introduced me to the song Viva La Vida by Coldplay, and the way you moved your hands and were right on time with the beat of the song. The memory made me smile.

These are famous quotes from the movie that I loved!

<u>Wizard</u>: What do you want to be in the world? I mean the whole world. What do you want to be? Close your eyes and think about that.
<u>August Rush</u>: Found.

<u>Louis Connelly</u>: [Louis explaining not giving up music to August] You never quit on your music. No matter what happens. Cuz anytime something bad happens to you, that's the one place you can escape to and just let it go. I learned it the hard way. And anyway, look at me. Nothing bad's gonna happen. You gotta have a little faith.

This quote means a lot to me because it is true. Music is one place where I can escape. This is what got me through hard times as a child and now as an adult.

After 17 times, I will not watch the movie again!

However, I want to add two more to this letter:

Charrisa: What do you want to be in the world? I mean the whole world. What do you want to be? Close your eyes and think about that.

Darlene: Loved. Like a woman should be loved by a man.}

You told me a few times (I won't say it exactly like you said it, but close), "Love is loving someone so much that you can destroy them, but you choose not to!" Wow, I thought that was a powerful statement.

You also told me on a couple of occasions that you would want me to look past your eyes into your soul to see what you saw in me. I thought then there must be something he sees that he likes or loves if he wants me to get close to his soul.

However, now what I see is the same person as my other ex's saw! A failure, a woman who just doesn't know how to love, a fool, and a worthless piece of used-up garbage that is only here to satisfy their desires.

Because I am a teacher, I will end with some positives. We start with positives then talk about the negatives, and end with positives. So here are the positives: You told me that you adored me! Well, I never knew what adored felt like. I find now that I like that word.

Then you gave me some feelings of worth. I was worth being treated like a lady. My self-esteem went up 100%.

Thank you...

For introducing me to Malt-O-Meal.

For coming to school, and letting me show-n-tell you.

For coming to church with me, to see and meet the people that really love me. I let you into my inner circle of friends and family, including my two children, Renae and Mike.

Then you gave me Christmas gifts that were very nice. The movie—you already know what it means to me. The sweater—made me feel beautiful; it fit my body nicely. I felt pretty in it. Silly, I know, however, that is what I felt. The perfume Lovely. I guess I like the name because it has love in it. It smelled good, too.

The most important gift you gave me was the poem. It is priceless! I will have it framed and will hang it in my bedroom because you saw the real me. You saw and even had my soul in your hands.

I am honored that you wrote a beautiful poem about me. Thanks for what you have given me.

What does this all mean to me? Well, trusting a man will be very hard to do, because now I know what destroy means! Because if the most amazing man on earth can convince you that you are worthy to be loved and he is the one who destroys you, then I know there is no way I would let just an ordinary man have my heart, or at least what is left of it.

I need to set boundaries for myself so I know when to say yes, when to say no, and to take control of my life!

As of today, I have made my last blanket, no more gifts of the heart. I think this one hurts the most because I don't see the reason to give gifts from the heart if the gifts that are given don't really make a difference in the people's lives that are important to me.

I will have to find something else that God would want me to do. I am not saving God for last because he is the least. It is because he should have been the most important one in my life. He should have been the one that made me smile, and helped me get through a bad day. God has never let me down; it is me that has let him down over and over, and I guess he is the one who really sees and knows, and more than anything loves the real me.

After writing the letter to Kelly, I needed to talk to someone who just might understand me. I knew who I would call because she knew how much I loved Jesus. I called Raquel and read to her what I had written to Kelly. With much prayer and the wisdom of a lady younger than I, I decided that I can't let Satan take away a ministry that I love. I will continue to bless the people that God puts in my path to bless. I guess you can say that I must really be learning, yet I feel that it is really God who is showing me that I am the *Most Amazing Woman*.

Kelly called and said he would be back in town soon and wanted to know if I hated him.

"No, I don't hate you, and I need to see you."

"Really?"

"Yes, I need to see you one last time."

So on a Tuesday night, I went to his apartment. I walked into the apartment carrying gifts, food and a box of Kleenex. "What are the Kleenex's for?" Kelly asked. I kind of laughed and said, "No special reason; it just feels like my heart is broken." We sat down on the couch. Kelly hugged me and I pulled back. I then asked, "Why?" He said when he met me that he didn't expect to fall in love with me.

I gave him the gifts to open. The first one was a toy drum. At our Christmas party, my Sunday school teacher's wife Cindy gave me and some others a drum. Then she told us why she gave us the drum:

Keep beating your faith drum. No matter what things look like, keep your faith going. Beating the drum was a way of expressing you're pressing on in faith, trusting God no matter what things look like.

Then I gave him a blanket. He opened his gifts. Then I read the note that I wrote him. He wiped his eyes. Then I asked if he had a CD player and he told me he could play it on the TV. However, he never did get it to work. He said we can use the one in his bedroom. I said that would work because I was going to perform for him. His eyebrows went up.

We went to the bedroom and I told him to sit there while I put the CD in and started the David Phelps music. The song that I interpreted to was *Mine*. The look on his face was priceless. After it was over, I said, "You took all of that and threw it away." We went back to the living room and I told him I really needed to leave.

"But you haven't eaten."

"That is okay, I don't feel like eating."

He took my hand and I sat down. He told me that he was sorry and still wanted to be my friend. I told him I could not promise anything right now.

Even though it was hard, I left there with no tears and I didn't cry. I had to be strong because deep down the thought that I had when we first met was true. I was not in the same league with Kelly.

Like before, Kelly came into my life for a reason. I found out that I was a person that could create boundaries later in life and I was an amazing woman.

After Kelly, I said there would be no other man. I was done. I started working on getting SHACK established and I started going to church more often and just being there to serve God.

On one of our Sunday school outings, a gentleman asked me if I was dating anyone. I told him, "NO!!!"

"I am done with men and I will be okay without them."

"Well let me ask you this, have you ever thought about thanking God for the man he is going to send you?"

"No," was my reply.

However, that night I started praying to God and thanking Him for the man He was going to send to me.

CHAPTER 18

Forgiveness

As early as I can remember, I have always had someone telling me that I needed to forgive people who have hurt me.

As a child I had a very hard time doing this. I blamed God for a whole lot. God made the heaven and earth. He made all kinds of animals, flowers, food and a million other things. However, he couldn't take care of one child. What was up with that? Did he not care how I was being mistreated? One day when I was having a very bad day, I screamed at God that I hated him, that he wasn't taking care of me. However, that same night when I was in bed with my other two sisters, I heard these words over and over, "I love you Darlene. I love you Darlene." I knew who was whispering those words.

It took a long time for me to realize that God loved me, that He wasn't causing all the bad to happen. He was there with me to see me through.

Be kind to one another, tenderhearted, forgiving one another, as God in Christ forgave you (Eph. 4:32, ESV).

The first person I had to forgive was me. I had to forgive myself for putting all the blame on God. I asked God to forgive me for always blaming him.

I forgave Raymond a long time before I forgave my mother. I know that this was because my mother should have been my protector. My mother should have put me before a man who was abusing her daughter.

I did forgive my mother and I talked to her one day at her nursing home and asked her why. She couldn't really give me an answer and I understood then that she thought in her mind that she hadn't done anything wrong.

"Mother please forgive me for being mad at you. Please forgive me for leaving home. Please forgive me."

There were no other words said. I turned around and left my mother standing there in her room. I then had to come to terms with the fact that I would have to honor my mother from a distance. That took a lot time.

I have asked forgiveness from the people that I could and prayed for the people that I couldn't reach to tell them I am sorry.

God loves us all and He does have a plan for us. I kept on believing that things would get better through every storm I was going through. I tried to stay positive when everything around me was negative.

God even had people come into my life at times when I needed them.

He also knew I made a lot of mistakes along the way. I was looking for love in all the wrong places. I thought if I was having sex, I was being loved. I thought if I was doing things to make people happy then I was loved. But I had to love myself first. I had to love that woman who was staring back at me in the mirror.

With God's love, grace and mercy, I know that He forgave me for all the mistakes I have made. God showed me that I was worthy to be loved.

God had a plan for me that I didn't understand until He sent me the man I was thanking him for in advance.

CHAPTER 19

I Kept on Believing

In spite of everything I been through, I kept on believing that things would get better for me. God didn't let me down.

When I was abused and raped, I got to move to another house where I didn't have to be scared and watch my back all the time.

When I didn't know I had a father, I found out that I did have one. His name was Elmer Boyd Stone.

When I was struggling in high school and failed the tenth grade, I went on to graduate from Central High School in Evansville, Indiana.

When I needed a man to listen to me there was Darrel Phelps. Still today I have the honor to speak to him from time to time.

When I didn't think I was good enough to be loved, I married my first husband who provided me with everything I wanted: a house, car and clothes.

When I wanted to have children to love and to be loved back, I had Renae and Mike.

When I didn't get what I thought I needed, I finally became single.

When I thought I needed a man, I found out that I didn't. I wanted a man. There's a big difference.

When I had a brain tumor, I had God, family and friends to see me through.

When I had a house fire, the house was put back together better than ever.

When I thought I was dating the most amazing man, I found out that I was the most amazing woman.

When I needed a family, I was invited to be a part of a great adoptive family.

When I was battling self-esteem and self-worth issues, my sister Kim asked me to be the keynote speaker at an AAWCC (American Association for Women in Community Colleges) conference. My topic was "The Real Me."

When I didn't think I was smart enough to go to college, I got my bachelor's degree.

When I thought I was used garbage and not worthy to be loved, God gave me a great gift that I was thanking him for in advance.

CHAPTER 20

SHACK

Being a single mother with a lot of time on my hands, sometimes I felt I wasn't needed anymore. Renae and Mike had their own lives and I was alone a lot. I have been blessed, and I needed and wanted to give back. I wanted something to do to serve others. So I founded SHACK. It stands for Serving Hearts Anytime Crisis Knocks. It was a blanket ministry, because these blankets have been given out of love! My goal is to give back to God for what he has given to me. I know that I will never be able to repay God, however I want to continue to serve God by making a difference for others.

The blankets may be given for different reasons; however, the main purpose is always the same – to spread God's love to others who might just need a little extra love.

When I was home and cleaning the house, I found this note that my daughter wrote about me. Of course, I cried.

Hello, my name is Renae and I am sure that a lot of you know who I am. I am the Founder's (Darlene Barlow) daughter. I wanted to share what I saw my mother doing through my eyes and share my thoughts.

My mother is a strong woman. She has battled many things in her life and I believe that is the reason that S.H.A.C.K has been created. My mother has been raped, been in bad marriages, survived a brain tumor, and has lost everything she has owned in a garage and house fire. If you could have picked a life to live, my mother's is not one to pick. However, she made something of herself and decided that her past was not going to decide her future.

If you think back as a child, I bet you can see that you clung to a blanket that was YOURS! Well, when we lost our possessions in the fire and when we thought our mother was not going to make it out from the surgery we clung to the blankets she had made us and felt like she was there. I believe that my mother wants to give people a blanket that they can cling to at night and feel comfort, and know that they can make it through another day.

My mother tells me all the time that she is going to be somebody someday. She already is. I see how she has transformed and I love her more and more every day.

SHACK was doing very well with lots of people wanting to help. We had a "tying party" where friends came together to tie the string in my garage. We didn't want people to have a crisis, but we were willing to give them a blanket of love in their time of need.

My first blanket was given to Eleanor. Even though there were many blankets given out, the first was very special to me. I gave the blanket to Jackie's sister and Terry's sister-n-law. Eleanor was also important to my family because when we had the house fire and I wanted my family to be together, we rented her house until our house could be repaired. God knew when I needed different people at different times.

Even when I was going through depression or a storm, it made me feel so much better when I could help others. It could have been because I wasn't focused on me and my issues. I was focused instead on the person who I was helping. I told my sister Kim that I will always serve God through SHACK. I found out, though, that sometimes God has a different plan for me.

CHAPTER 21

Never Say Never

One day while I was lying on my couch watching a movie, my sister Connie called me.

"Hello."

"I found a man for you."

"Oh, you did?"

She told me to get on the computer and go to www.craigslist.com. To say the least, I laughed out loud! I went to my computer and the website. Together we laughed about all the ads for males looking for a mate.

After that conversation, I started thinking that I might try a different singles online dating service. So one day when I was home alone and really kind-of depressed, I got on the website www.singles.net. I thought it couldn't hurt just to look. It was safer than going to a bar. I also found out dating a Christian man is not always a good thing either, because they might know all the right things to say and know scriptures by heart; but if the mind and heart were not connected together, that person might not be who I was looking for.

Since I was a single mom again, I didn't want to have to pay for the upgraded features on the dating site. I was able to click on a profile for free, and if that person was interested, he could write me back. The very first guy I clicked on wrote me back. *Whew, that was fast!* In the back on my mind, however, I considered it to be a God thing, so I took a leap of faith and replied back to him. The process of communicating on the website was taking too long, and I am not a very patient person. So, I asked him if he wanted my email address. He said yes!

I started talking to Steve Snow. *Steve Snow. That has a nice sound to it. I have always loved snowmen and even collected snowmen. I think I would like to get to know this snowman.*

Steve and I started writing back and forth and sharing information about ourselves. Steve was a widower and had two sons—Nathaniel, age 12, and Nicholas, age 11. He lived in Crestwood, Kentucky, and was an electrical engineer.

A red flag should have gone up because I said I would never date a man with children under the age of 18. I must remind everyone that you should never say never! I had failed at blended families not once, but twice. However, this one would be different. There would not be an ex that I would have to deal with.

I met Steve in the summer when I was off work. He asked if I wanted to meet. I had already made plans to go with Tonya to Ashland, so I told Steve that we had to wait and meet at another time.

Tonya, Rick and I went down to Kim's house to help clean her garage out. I was excited about going to Kim and Dean's place. We had a nice time helping them clean this huge garage out. This gave me time to spend with them so I didn't have to be alone at the house. Kim and Dean's place was awesome. It was in the country.

The weekends always go by too fast. Before you knew it, we were heading back home. But I wasn't sad this time. I think it was because I was talking to Steve. It just felt good to talk to someone, even if it was through texts and email.

I texted Steve on the way back and told him I would be home around 5:00. He asked if I wanted to meet. I said sure, but it would be about 6:00 before I could meet him. We decided to meet at the Cracker Barrel on Bardstown Road since it was about half way for both of us. I was a little nervous but I told my daughter where I was going and who I was meeting just in case I didn't come back. No, I didn't tell her "in case I didn't come back," but I sure did think it.

When I first saw Steve, I thought, "Well, he looks like the picture." He put his name on the waiting list, but we only had to wait a few minutes.

He ordered fish. *Yuck! I won't be kissing him tonight.* I ordered my usual kid's grilled chicken with hash brown casserole and sweet tea. We ate and talked about our lives just like we did in the emails.

After we finished, he asked if I wanted to take a ride and I said sure. I walked to his car. It was an old car, a '94 Chevy Cavalier. Steve put the top down and we were on our way, cruising with the top down. We ended up in Bardstown and went to the Stephen Foster Story. We didn't plan that, but it just worked out.

On that night, you got to pick what you wanted to pay for the tickets. Steve said, "Well how much?" to the lady. She said, "Anything. Some people give a dollar, some give five." So Steve gave a ten.

We found our seats and sat down to watch the show. As we sat there, Steve took my hand and held it, which I thought was nice. Steve got two phone calls from one of his sons, Nathaniel. He asked his dad if he was having fun.

After the show, Steve drove me back to my car. It was an awesome first date that I didn't want to end. However, I had to work the next day at my summer job. Every chance we got, we would text each other and call when we could.

One day after work that summer, I thought I would show up at Steve's house. However, I got lost and had to call Steve and tell him I was lost! It was pouring down rain. I was lost somewhere in Crestwood, so Steve said he would come get me since he knew where I was. He asked if he could bring his son with him and I said sure.

They were there in about ten minutes. Steve got out, walked over and asked if I wanted to go eat. I did, so I got out of my car and got into his SUV. I turned in the seat and said, "Hi, I'm Darlene." The young boy said, "Hi, I'm Nathaniel."

We went to Cracker Barrel again. We talked about general stuff since Nathaniel was there with us. Nathaniel told me that his brother, Nicholas, was camping with a friend. *Well, at least I know they like to camp.*

As we were almost finished with our dinner, Steve said, "I don't mind you coming to my house. However, I must warn you it is real messy." I said, "That's okay. My house is messy, too." Nathaniel added, "I don't think anyone's house could be bad as ours." I didn't really know what to say then. I knew their mother had passed away, but that was over a year ago. I told Steve and Nathaniel it was up to them if they wanted me to come to their house.

I followed them to their house. I thought it was back in the sticks as I was following them, but then we turned into a nice subdivision. When I pulled into the driveway, my thought was that the house looked okay from the outside so the inside couldn't be that bad. *Oh my goodness! I was so wrong.* The house was terrible. There was stuff everywhere. Steve had to move things so I could sit on the couch.

Nathaniel went and got on the computer. Steve and I just sat and watched TV. After Nathaniel went to bed, we talked. Steve said he was sorry about the house. He told me his late wife was a hoarder. She bought everything.

The house wasn't like the TV show where folks have all the garbage. The house had stuff everywhere and it was brand new stuff. I asked Steve what he was doing with it all. He said he wanted to have a yard sale. My thought was, "He could open a store!" I didn't stay long that night. As I drove back home, I was thinking that God put me in Steve's life to get his house clean.

Over the next week, we talked a lot and texted like crazy. I wanted to know things. I asked a lot of questions. I wanted to really get to know this "snow" man.

Steve decided to have a yard sale so I agreed to help get things ready. Steve priced most of the items. The room that had all the stuff for the yard sale was a bedroom. When he opened the door, I was amazed by all the stuff on the bed plus everything around the room. I asked Steve if I could give him my opinion. I must say I do give it a lot. He said yes. I told him I would concentrate on getting all this extra stuff out of his house!

The yard sale was on Saturday and Steve made $200.00. That was not enough. I thought that the reason we didn't sell much was due to the location. We needed to have the yard sale in Louisville. So, I began planning the next yard sale.

I was enjoying getting to know Steve and the boys. I met Nicholas at the yard sale. I think the boys took care of each other because their mother was sick a lot. The boys were quiet and didn't say a whole lot. When they did, I listened.

When I got home and thought about Steve and the boys, I remembered the advice that I got from my assistant Ms. Pat. She told me before I married Johnny how hard it is to be married to someone with children. I didn't listen to her that time nor the next time when I married Johnny for the second time. So, here I was dating a man with two boys. What was I thinking? Or was I thinking at all? There was no rushing into anything. Time would tell where this would go. As I was sitting there, I talked to God:

> *It's me again I want to thank you for sending Steve to me. However, I didn't think I needed to put restrictions on what I wanted. I thought you knew that I don't do well with blended families. I wish I knew your plans for me. Please be with me and all that I do with Steve. Please help me keep you first in my life. Amen.*

After praying, I got on the phone and called Connie. I told her about Steve and how the house was and that I thought Steve was in my life so I could help him clean his house.

We planned to have the next yard sale at my house. Steve and I had more people to help and we told everyone. When I told Steve about SHACK, he told me that since I was helping him with the yard sale, he would give a portion of the sale to SHACK.

At that yard sale we made over $400.00. The house looked better, but we still had a whole lot of stuff. All my family came. Kim came from Ashland, and Connie, Tonya, Mom and Dad, and many cousins and friends came, as well. We all felt that we still didn't have the right location for the sale. I stressed to them how much stuff was still left. Connie asked me if the house was full of stuff.

"Yes, Connie, we haven't gotten all the stuff out of the one bedroom that we want to clean so the boys can have their own room."

We thanked everyone who helped. I was so tired. We loaded up Steve's trailer and Steve and the boys went home. I told Steve I would be back out to his house after church. Steve asked me if he could go to church with me. That was music to my ears. I told Steve I went to the first service. He said he would see me there.

Steve and the boys came to church and we left after the service. It felt good sitting by Steve in church. I always said, "I am not going to settle for less than the best," and the best would be a man sitting by me in church.

We went back out to Steve's house. We ate lunch and got right back into going through stuff in the room. This was taking a lot more time than I thought it would. We had to check every bag and if it was a purse we had to check it, too, because Steve's late wife would put money everywhere. One purse had $20.00 in it.

Later that day while we were taking a break, the doorbell rang. The dogs started barking and Steve went to the door and opened it. It was Connie, Doug, Tonya and Rick. I gave them a tour of the house. When we went downstairs, Connie confessed that she didn't believe me when I had told her about all the stuff. She had to come and see it for herself.

So the planning began. We needed to have a huge yard sale. My family brought their vehicles out and we moved stuff to Connie's house. We were going to have a yard sale in front of the fire house on Preston Highway.

We had a lot of family help us that day. We had tables and tents and trailers. We had a cash drawer. We had a toy section, housewares, clothes, and fine things like collections of plates. We had so many dolphin decorations that I got sick of looking at them. I even used to collect dolphins. However, not anymore.

My fear was that I was doing all this work for Steve and when the job was done that Steve would break up with me. My sister wrote this note for Steve to sign. It said:

"Steve will date Darlene as long as the sisters want him to."

It was really a cute note and he signed it. That day was more like a family reunion. It was a lot of work, but so worth it. Steve made $4322.00. Now, that was a yard sale! It was enough to pay off one credit card.

There is no way we could have done all that without the family helping us. I was very proud of my family for their hard work. Not just for the yard sale but for helping clean the house, too. Most of all, it showed what a real family life looks like.

We continued working on the house. We got the room cleaned out and my brother-in-law, Rick, came out and painted the rooms for the boys while they were gone to their first church camp. When they came back from camp they were very happy with their rooms.

Dating Steve was awesome! He was so nice to me. He cooked for me. He kissed me. He held my hand out in public. I was falling for him. But in the back of my head, I was scared. I didn't want to be a failure again. I wanted to be loved like a woman should be loved. I opened my mouth and was willing to insert my foot to say what I wanted to say to Steve.

We were sitting by the pool and I was quiet, which doesn't happen often. Steve asked me if something was wrong. I told him no, not really.

"What does that mean?" Steve looked a little worried.

"Well, I told you that I failed at a blended family not once, but twice. I just don't think I have it in me to go through that again. I know we don't even know where this relationship is going. However, if we see that it is going somewhere, would you think about going to counseling if we continue to date?"

Steve thought for what seemed like forever to me. Then he said yes, I think that would be good for us. Then Steve kissed me.

Whew, that was too easy. Maybe he is agreeing to keep me around. Maybe I am good enough for Steve. Even though I tried to keep the negative thoughts out of my head, they seemed to get in there one way or the other.

One day, Steve took me to meet his mother. She was a very sweet lady. She was in the nursing home and her husband, Royce (Steve's stepfather), was praying for her strength to come back so she could go home.

Steve's father passed away when he was thirty-five years old. Steve also had a sister, Trish, who was in a nursing home due to an accident. I realized Steve sure has had a lot of heartache in the past few years, and I thought that maybe I could bring joy to Steve life.

A few days later, Steve received a call that they were taking his mother to the hospital. He texted me while I was at work. I went to the hospital after work. His mother was in the emergency room and looked really bad. Steve and Royce both looked very worried.

While they were waiting to get a room, I asked if there was anything I could do. Steve asked me if I could get Nathaniel and Nicholas for him. He didn't want to leave his mother.

Steve told me to take his car to get the boys, because I had a small truck. I told him I loved him and would be back as soon as I could. He said he loved me, too, and to drive safely. As I was leaving to go pick up the boys, I had a gut instinct that this was going to be a sad time for Steve.

When I got to the house, the boys were already home from school. I told them what was going on. The boys were quiet. We went through a drive-thru to get the boys something to eat. Nicholas asked me if his grandmother was going to die. I told him I didn't know. Nicholas said he hated it when people die. I told him I did, too.

When we got to the hospital, they had moved Steve's mom to a room. It was a huge room. Some of Steve's family came up. Royce was so sad. He loved his wife so much. He told me the first time he met Frances he thought she was the most beautiful woman, and she still is.

Connie and Doug came up later that night. They ended up taking Nathaniel and Nicholas home with them because Steve and I were going to stay the night. My gut instinct was correct. They didn't think Frances was going to make it through the night.

A lot of family members came and went through the evening. Frances' sister Beulah and her husband Jack came up. I asked if I could get anything for Steve and Royce, but they said no. Sometimes Steve would sit at the end of his mother's bed and other times he would come and sit by me. He held my hand and thanked me for being there with him. I smiled and told him I was where I was supposed to be. Frances passed away in the early morning. She was surrounded by her family who loved her.

I followed Steve to get Nathaniel and Nicholas, then I had to go to work. I hated to leave Steve. I told him I would be back as soon as I could. When I went to work, I told Michelle and Ms. Pat what had happened. They told me I should be there for Steve. So I went to talk to Dr. Young and asked if I could have a few days off. I still had my personal days available, so I took them.

I drove back to Steve's house. I felt so sorry for him. I knew how it felt to lose a parent. There are really no words to say. So I just hung around him. Later that day we were going to meet Royce at the funeral home.

Steve went to bed to get some sleep. I just cleaned the kitchen. I kept busy and tried to be quiet. But the more I tried to be quiet, it seemed like I was making more noise. So I laid down on the couch and went to sleep.

Steve woke me up around 1:00 in the afternoon, and I couldn't believe I had slept that long. Steve had already showered and dressed. I got up and asked him if he had an extra tooth brush. He did.

We left to meet Royce. I tried to get Steve to eat something, but he said he wasn't hungry. He did drink some coffee. This was going to be a long afternoon.

I was not prepared for the funeral home. Steve's Aunt Beulah and Uncle Jack were there along with Royce. We met with the funeral director. They went over the ad that would be in the paper. Then we were directed to the room that had all the caskets.

I would have never thought there would be so many to choose from. It was kind of creepy walking around those caskets. I wasn't afraid because my friend Sheila was an embalmer. In the past, I would visit her at the funeral home where she worked. However, I had never gone in a room like that.

After we made all the funeral arrangements, we went out to eat with everyone. They all shared stories about Frances. It was nice listening to the stories. There were tears. The love for Frances was shown in the stories and on the faces of her son, husband and sister.

After we left there, Steve asked me if I would come back to his house and stay with him. I said, "Yes, but I need to go get clothes from my house and other things I might need." I really didn't know how long I would be staying. So we went and I packed for a few days.

I talked to Renae and Mike and told them what was going on. I let them know that I would be staying with Steve for a few days. They didn't give me a hard time which, I was thankful for.

With the arrangements made, we didn't really have a lot to do. Steve worked on a slide show for his mom. I didn't want to smother him, but I would still go in the kitchen where he was working and check on him. Sometimes I would see tears. Sometimes he would tell me about the picture he was scanning. I suggested the song *I Can Only Imagine* for the background music.

I stayed by Steve's side through the visitation and the funeral. I made sure Nathaniel and Nicholas were okay and listened when they needed to talk. One of Steve's cousins, Phyllis, told me that Steve and the boys had it bad the past few years. She said that Steve's wife passed away on their twentieth anniversary, his sister got hurt, and now his mother passed away. Phyllis thanked me for being there for Steve.

After the funeral, we went to Royce's church to have lunch. We celebrated Frances' life. I knew God had put me in Steve's life for more than cleaning his house. He put me in Steve's life for Steve to lean on me through this hard time.

That night I went back to Steve's house. We ate a light supper and watched a movie with the boys. When the boys went to bed, Steve thanked me for being there for him and the boys.

The next morning, I would be going back home. It was also my birthday. We were out of school because it was a professional development day. I was planning to go to the St. James Art Show.

When I got up, the boys were also just getting up. They were very quiet getting ready and eating breakfast. Nathaniel asked if I would be there when they got home. I told them I didn't know and that I was going to an art fair.

Nathaniel and Nicholas both wished me a happy birthday and said good bye. They went out the door to wait for the bus. Steve went with them which I thought was odd because he didn't do that the day before. I could hear them talking, but couldn't make out what they were saying. After the bus came, Steve came back inside.

I asked Steve if everything was okay. He said it was. He got me a cup of coffee and sat down by me. He said "I want to thank you for all you have done for me and the boys." He also said, "With all you have done for us I know I want you in my life. Will you be my wife?"

Oh my goodness. I didn't expect that. I replied, "Yes." Steve then told me what he and the boys were discussing on the front steps. He was asking Nathaniel and Nicholas if it was okay if he asked me to marry him. They both said yes, and Nathaniel told him good luck!

Steve said, "I don't have a ring for you, but, we can go look for one today." To say the least, I didn't go to the art show.

I called Renae and Mike and told them first. Then I called my mom and dad and told them. Lastly I called my sisters.

Mike and Renae

along with

Nathaniel and Nicholas

Request the honor of your presence,

at the marriage of their parents.

Darlene Barlow

to

Steven Snow

CHAPTER 22

Growing in Love

On December 13, 2009, I married my very own snowman. I am more blessed than I deserve. Steve loves me just I am. Steve is very supportive of everything I do.

Has our life been storm free? Not on your life. Sometimes we have a dusting of snow. Sometimes we have snow storms and other times we have a full blown blizzard. Sometimes I would like to have a perfect marriage with no storms, but when we are in a storm we grow closer to God. We need His power and strength to endure.

We watched Mike go off to boot camp for the United States Army. With the help of my family and Mike's girlfriend Amber, we got through the five months. Then we all got to see Mike propose to Amber at the graduation. Amber said yes. Amber has already made a difference in our lives, bringing our family closer together.

Our family and Renae's boyfriend Rob helped Renae move into her first apartment. Renae is gaining her independence as a young adult. I am very proud of her wanting to be a teacher and to help educate children.

We have helped Mike move into his first house and we are preparing for a wedding. Mike and Amber will be getting married this year.

Nathaniel is going to graduate this year and soon will be going to college. Nicholas will be a junior in the fall and is still confusing me with all the things he talks about. He loves the computer and is always trying to figure out how something works.

Steve encourages me to stay real to myself. To stay real to myself, I had to take a lot of masks off. The masks were: the victim of child abuse, the victim of rape, the victim of feeling unloved, and the victim of low self-esteem.

I started truly relying on God. All through my life I knew about Him, but just didn't really know Him. Even though I was baptized at the age of fifteen, it felt as though I was missing something. When I turned 40, I rededicated my life to God. That was twelve years ago and it made a huge change in my whole attitude.

Taking off the masks empowered me and gave me the desire to read more and understand what I am reading. Once again, I must mention the book by John McCloud and Henry Townsend called *Boundaries*. While reading this book, I discovered I didn't really have any boundaries in my life. I had lived my life always doing for others, trying to make everyone else happy. In doing this, I was making my own life miserable and dying on the inside. I wanted everyone to like me, so I set no boundaries. Setting boundaries as an older adult was and still is hard. People had come to rely on me always giving, but I was giving pieces of myself away. In order to survive and become real, I had to set boundaries for myself. Knowing when to give and when to ask for help means I have finally found the real me. This book helped me to set boundaries in all areas of my life and I encourage you to read it.

Setting boundaries for myself, making confident decisions and taking off the masks has allowed me to grow as a person to find the real me, who knows without a doubt that "I can do all things through Christ who strengthens me."

I am proud to say I am a child of God, a wife, a mother, a daughter, sister and friend, who has a college degree. I am a real person who struggles every day to not wear a mask.

Steve loves me so much that he went with me to tour my childhood elementary school. The school was sold to a contractor who was going to turn it into different kinds of offices. He was so nice to let the former students see the building.

That day I walked up the thirty concrete steps as the teenager had done so many times before. However, I walked down the thirty steps as a grown up survivor.

This is the end of my life story to date, or so I thought. When I finished writing, I was utterly relieved. It felt like a burden was lifted off my shoulders. However, there was something not right about it.

I sent a copy of my book to a few friends and a couple of family members. I was even bold enough to send a copy to Dr. Young. All of them said pretty much the same thing—I needed to find an editor and get the story published.

Early one morning, I went out and sat on our deck. I thought about the book and felt that it really didn't matter if it were published or not. The words I kept hearing in my head were, "It is not finished." I then said out loud:

"Not finished!? Are you serious? What more do I have to go through for it to be finished?"

As I sat there, my wonderful husband opened the door, walked outside and asked:

"Who are you talking to?"

"God."

Steve handed me my coffee and turned around and walked back into the house.

I turned my head to both sides to make sure no one else was listening to me talk out loud. Then I said a quick prayer for Steve not to think he married a crazy woman and have me committed to a mental health institution.

Afterwards, I got up and went back into the house to drink coffee and to watch the news.

As we watched WDRB news, we heard a story about a hidden hero named Leslie Thomas who co-founded SOAR which stands for "Survivors of Abuse Restored."

"Well there is my answer."

"Your answer to what question?"

"The answer to the question I was asking God."

I didn't even let him ask the next question because I already knew what he was going to ask.

"When you brought my cup of coffee you heard me say 'Not finished? Are you serious? What more do I have to go through for it to be finished?' I think it has something to do with this lady Leslie Thomas and the Hidden Hero award. We will have to watch the rest of the news."

I still didn't know why my book wasn't finished at that very moment. But I knew God wanted me to hear about SOAR because I still had issues I had not dealt with.

CHAPTER 23

Anger and Depression

Anger and depression were the reason my book wasn't finished. This is very hard to write about. I think it is because I have struggled with depression almost all of my life. But there was something that I was missing.

I know some people might not agree with me when I say a child can have depression. I know this because, as a child, I did. I didn't know the term depression, but I was sad a lot. In some ways, I thought it was normal to be sad because my sad days were more often than my happy days.

Sure, most children have disappointments in their life. No one's life is perfect. But being sexually and mentally abused is not something any child or any adult should go through.

I had so much pressure on me as a child. I was keeping a secret and wanted to tell, but then I was scared of the outcome. I wanted my mother to be proud of me, but

I felt inside that I could never make her happy. I was a disappointment to her, but I didn't know why.

When the rape happened, my emotions and feelings were all over the place. I felt an overwhelming cloud of sadness over me. I was hurting inside even though I looked like a normal teenager on the outside. I was screaming inside for help, but no one heard.

I started going to a therapist at the age of fifteen. I have been to so many doctors and on so much medicine that I could be a spokesperson for a medical company. The guilt that was put on me because Raymond went to jail was wrong. He should have gone to jail. I thought my mother should have gone to jail, too, because she allowed the abuse to happen. That thought conflicted with the sense that I should honor my mother.

With Steve at my side, we waited and watched the story on Leslie Thomas and SOAR. We listened to ladies who were willing to share what SOAR meant to them. After listening to the news story, I went to my office and cried. I cried because I learned I was not alone. I cried because there was a place I could go to talk to people who knew what I had been going through.

I sent Lindsay Allen an email thanking her for doing the story and she wrote me back giving me the contact information for the co-founder of SOAR. The very next day I called the number I was given and left a message. The same day Leslie Thomas called me. I told her I saw the story on the TV.

"Is this a Bible-based program?"

"Yes it is. But you don't have to be a Christian to come to our classes."

"I am a Christian."

I just wanted it to be Bible-based. She gave me the information and encouraged me to come to an open door meeting on Thursday night. Unfortunately, I already had something planned for that night. Then she said:

"We will be starting a new class next Monday night at 6:30 p.m. You are more than welcome to come."

"That is great and I will be there."

Before I knew it, I was sitting at a round table with six other women and two facilitators.

This is where I learned that I had anger towards my mother. The depression that I had was me being mad at my mother and not voicing it and turning the anger inward. This was the thing I was missing. I was ANGRY!!! I was so mad at my mother. I was mad at her for not protecting me. I was mad at her for enabling Raymond. I was mad at her for blaming me for things that I didn't have any control over. I WAS A CHILD!

I did say that I forgave Raymond, my mother and many other people who had abused me. This is when I learned that it wasn't my fault. However, what I said in my head had not connected to my heart. I had forgiven them intellectually, but not in my whole being. I needed to write

one more letter to Raymond. With the help from SOAR
and Cathy Jo Summers I was able to:

Raymond,

*I am writing this letter because I wanted you to
know what you took from me as a child.*

*As a child of five, you put fear into my mind. You
made me watch over my shoulder all the time. You
made me keep secrets which I should have been a
care-free child without any worries.*

I feel like you stole my childhood from me!

*You raped me while I was in the bed with my niece.
Even though the rape was terrible and being
molested since five wasn't enough for you to take
from me, then you had to brush my teeth with
comet.*

What right did you have to do that?

*So, every time I look in the mirror I am reminded
of my abuse. For that I have hated you! For me to
recover from the past, I need to forgive you.*

*I did forgive you a very long time ago for the rape
and molesting me.*

*But, I never forgave you for brushing my teeth
with Comet.*

*So as of today, March 22nd, I forgive you for
brushing my teeth with Comet.*

With God's love and my husband loving me no matter what I look like, I can move on and accept me as me.

Since you are no longer on this earth, I will bury this note at the cross in my front yard.

You won't have control over my mind anymore.

I am praying for Mercy and Grace over your soul and praying you were forgiven and accepted Christ in your life before your death.

With no hatred inside,

Darlene

It is also at SOAR where I learned that I was known as a *caregiver*. This means I go out of my way to do things for people so they will like me. It also showed me why I was always searching for love, sometimes in the wrong places. I found out I had to be able to heal from the inside out. I also learned that a little girl needed to be rescued and that I, as an adult, needed to be restored. This is where I heard that I was not alone.

I said in one of the sessions that I wished I had known of SOAR fourteen years ago. However, I wasn't ready fourteen years ago. I would not have listened then. I was where God wanted me to be. It took SOAR to help me connect my mind to my heart.

Ever since I lost my teeth, I hated the face that was looking back at me in the mirror because my mouth was a constant reminder of my childhood and the abuse I endured. It wasn't until July 28, 2014, that I stopped hating myself when I looked in a mirror.

As I was sitting by the campfire at Butler State Park in Carrollton, Kentucky, while Steve was asleep in our pop-up, I had a flashback to a time when I was sitting at the gravesite of my father. I was talking to my father and God. I asked God to be with me every step of my life and He has never let me down. God loved me then and He still loves me today.

Then I got up and walked to the restroom for the last time of the night. As I was standing there in front of the mirror, I smiled really big. I said to myself:

"Wow, where did that beautiful smile come from?"

"It has always been there," I heard.

Now whenever I look in the mirror I see a smile. I have even started taking selfies of me with everyone and anything. My mouth doesn't define who I am; my heart, soul, and the relationship I have with God does.

EPILOGUE: MOTHER AND ME

I must tell you there is no way I could have written this next chapter without the help of God. *A Girl Named Darlene* has been sitting ready to be published for several months, but something was keeping it from final publication. Then the phone rang.

God knew! I give God all the Praise and Glory for all He has done for me in my life. I could not be who am I today if I didn't have him as my Lord and Savior.

I received a called from Terry that our mother was in the hospital. Terry said, "Mom has cancer." I was upset only because listening to my brother's worry and grief bothered me tremendously.

"Terry, I am sorry to hear this."

"After I get home and take a shower, Jamie and I will be heading over there to the hospital."

"What time do you think you will get there?

"I would say around 6:30."

"I will see you there."

"Okay, I love you sis."

As soon as I got off the phone, I looked at Steve and said, "That was Terry and he said Mother is in the hospital with cancer. I need you to take me over to Floyd Memorial hospital please." Steve looked at me with this funny look on his face like he was trying to figure out why I was going to the hospital.

There have been times during our marriage when I had similar calls and didn't go. I didn't go because the pain was still raw and because mother and I were still at odds about my past. I was still learning to honor my mother from a distance. I can understand why Steve was both confused and concerned about me going to the hospital.

I went to our room and sat on the bed feeling like I didn't know what I wanted to do. I knew what I had just told Terry, but I didn't know why I even said that to my brother in the first place. It was like I didn't have any control over what I was saying.

Dear God,

I am at a loss about what I need to do. I am not sure how mother will be. I don't have any idea if her attitude will be nice or mean. Please be with me as I walk this path that will be hard to walk.

I got up, grabbed my overnight bag, and packed pajama's pants, a t-shirt, and my medicine container. Then Steve walked in the room and saw me get my glasses, eye mask and my pillow.

"What are you doing?"

"I am taking some things with me in case I spend the night."

"Why would you do that?"

"I am not sure why I am doing this. I feel like I should do this even if it is for Terry."

As Steve drove me to the hospital, I was still thinking about what I was doing and I also kept praying. When we reached the hospital, Steve came around the car and took my hand. I told him to leave my bag in the car until I went in to assess the situation. He said okay.

I was a little nervous entering the hospital, but not like I thought I would be. As we walked into my mother's room, I saw Terry and Jamie. I then saw my mother in the hospital bed. She didn't look like my mother. She was swollen, had bruises all over her arms, and had an oxygen tube going in her nose.

"Hi, mother."

My mother looked at me and laughed and giggled. She couldn't remember my name, so she called me baby and said, "You brought your honey." I said yes.

We sat and we made small talk. A nurse came in and changed an IV bag and another bag. I asked her what was in the bag and the nurse explained that it was mother's chemo. Terry said that Larry would be coming in the morning to stay and talk to the doctor. I then asked:

"Mother would you like for me to spend the night with you?"

"If you want to."

I asked Steve to go and get my things from the car. Terry, Jamie, and Steve didn't stay very long after that because mother was getting tired and it was getting late.

When I talked to my mother, I had to talk very loudly because her hearing was bad. I knew what she meant when she said, "I left my do hinkies at home." Mother forgot her hearing aids. I just laughed at some of the words she said.

My mother would drift in and out of sleep as she was watching TV. I was writing down everything that had happened since I got the phone call from Terry. Mother asked:

"Baby, why are you writing with your right hand?"

"I got hurt at work and I have real bad migraines and when they are real bad it affects my left hand so much that I cannot write with it."

"Will it get better and healed?"

"I sure hope so! I've been praying. Mother, I have written a book about my life."

"I was never good to you."

"That is okay. I forgive you."

"Good. I love you."

"I love you, too."

At that moment, there were tears running down my face. That was the first time in forty-five years that my mother told me she loved me. This time, I knew she meant it and I believed it.

As I looked over at my mother, she had drifted backed to sleep. I sat there in awe of what had just taken place. I knew then why I had come to the hospital. This was God's plan. It was no accident that I packed a bag or I didn't have a migraine that would make me sick enough to be confined to my bed. I just kept on writing in my journal because I didn't want to forget anything. Due to my post-concussion syndrome, I am prone to short term memory loss. I wanted to remember this moment for the rest of my life.

Mother did wake up a little bit when the nurse came in for the last time to check on her and gave her the evening medicine she takes. Mother looked at me and asked, "Are you okay?" I told her I was doing great. I had changed into pajamas and they brought me a recliner to sleep in. Mother said, "Okey-dokey, I am going to sleep."

I continued to write in my journal, and I texted Steve to let him know everything was okay. Then I sat in the chair and just listened to my mother breathe. I realized that I didn't want my mother to die. My mother just told me she loves me. I thought it sounded like music to my ears!

I don't understand why all that blood has to be taken in the middle of the night. The light was turned on and the lab person came over to tell my mother that it was time to take her blood. She said it again, "I am here to take your blood." My mother, barely awake, quietly uttered, "I am not supposed to be here; I am supposed to be in Heaven." I got up out of my chair and walked around to where the lab person was and said:

> "Mother, this lady wants to take your blood for a test."
>
> "I am not supposed to be here; I am supposed to be in Heaven."
>
> "Not tonight Mother."
>
> "Not tonight?"
>
> "Not tonight."
>
> "Okey-dokey."

The lab person tried to get blood, but mother's veins were too bad. She will have them get her blood in the morning.

My mother went back to sleep and I went back to my chair until around eight when the shift changed.

Larry got to the hospital right when they delivered mother's breakfast. As the food came in, so did the doctor. The doctor was very nice and talked to the three of us. He thought mother would be going home the next day. As the doctor was leaving I asked if I could have a minute of his time and walked out into the hall with him. I explained that my brother Larry has power of attorney and needs to be present when any bad news is shared or decisions are made about treatment options. Apparently some of the hospital staff had told my mother things without informing Larry. The doctor was very apologetic and he assured that this would be noted and followed in the future.

I asked Larry how long he was going to stay. After learning he could stay for a little longer, I decided to call Steve and have him pick me up. I had no sleep the night before that I was starting to feel bad.

When I got in the car, I started talking non-stop and told Steve everything that took place. As we were driving home, I got a text from Terry that read, "Call me." As soon as I heard Terry's voice, I could tell that he had been or still was crying.

> "Larry just called and the cancer is really bad. As of right now, just the three of us know. I have to get back to work. I love you sis."

> "I love you brother."

Steve offered to take me back to the hospital if I wanted to be there with Larry, but I knew Larry was headed to work soon and I needed to get some sleep.

I know cancer is hard on anyone who hears the "C" word. When I hear the word, I always think of the worst-case scenario. Telling our other siblings about the news was not going to be easy. Terry, Larry and I were worried about our sister Linda because her husband had passed away just six months ago. We also worried about our older sister, Tina because we were not sure she could handle the news about mother's illness. There is also our brother Paul who we hadn't seen in a while and weren't sure how to contact.

I called Renae and Mike right away and told them about their grandmother. They both said they were sorry to hear she had cancer.

It doesn't take long for information to get out in our family. In some ways it was good because everyone knew my mother was sick and could start praying for her. There was a down side, however. They started planning mother's funeral before she was even dead! I had to make a few calls to take care of the drama before things got out hand.

I thought to myself *I am taking care of my mother*. It wasn't a bad thought; it was a very good one. It let me see the relationship between my mother and I in a different way.

Renae picked me up one day to take me shopping and get me out of the house. Renae said:

> "Mom can I ask you something and it won't make you upset or mad for me asking?"

I thought to myself *that is a very loaded question* and wondered how I should answer it. I said, "I will try not to get mad or upset. But if I don't like the conversation, I will say I don't want to talk about it."

> "Okay. Well I know you will be upset when your mother passes away maybe a little bit. But, wow, I never expected this kind of reaction when you found out she was sick. What changed?"

> "Whew! I didn't know what you were going to ask or tell me." With great joy and excitement, I said, "But Renae, let me tell you what happened at the hospital..."

I told Renae everything that took place including how my mother told me, "I love you." Renae said:

> "I understand now and it makes sense. But mom, if you go around her and she is mean again, you can't take it personal. God gave you a gift. Plus, you know how chemotherapy can make you sick and your mother is seventy-five."

> "Where in the world did I get this wise young lady from? Renae, you are right. God did give me a gift and I will forever be grateful.

We had a wonderful mother and daughter day.

Terry called me and said Larry told him they are going to start mother on chemotherapy and radiation. I felt thankful that she was going to get treatment. We made more phone calls sharing the positive news, and I posted on Facebook asking for prayers for my mother during her chemotherapy and radiation.

The next week I got a called from Larry. He wanted to know if I could take mother to her next appointment to set up her treatments. I agreed because I was off work and happy to spend more time with her. I had to ask Steve to drive because at the time I wasn't able to. As always Steve said yes.

When Steve and I picked up my mother and took her to the appointment, we learned that the radiation would start immediately and the treatments would be every day for 30 days. My mother asked, "Will I lose my hair?" The nurse practitioner said, "Your hair will thin out, but you will not lose your hair." That made my mother happy.

When we left the doctor's appointment, Steve and I took mother to lunch at Kentucky Fried Chicken. As we drove back to the nursing home, I turned around and looked at my mother because she was so quiet. She was sleeping. Once we got mother back safety to the nursing home, she thanked us for the trip.

As Steve and I were driving home, all I could think about is my disbelief that I had made up with my mother.

I took my mother to doctor. Plus, my mother was nice to me! The feeling of being around my mother when there is no meanness, malice, or unkind words was more than a blessing.

After several radiation treatments, mother was scheduled to start chemotherapy. Larry called me asking if I could help take mother to her chemo appointments, because someone needed to stay with her for several hours. As always, Steve was very supportive and agreed to drive Mother and I to and from the chemo treatments. He did, however, make me promise that I would take care of myself, too. The doctor told us the first day will be the longest, so I suggested that Steve drop me off then I could call him when mother was almost finished. Larry was going to meet me there the first day.

My sister Linda and I had been texting or talking on the phone ever since we learned about mother's cancer. Luckily Linda had warned me that mother was losing her hair so that I would not be surprised when I saw her that day. Still, when I walked back to the room where mother was waiting, I wasn't expecting to see my mother with a wig on.

"Mother, you have a new look. Are you making a fashion statement?"

"What?"

"I like your new look."

My mother started laughing and said, "I like it, too."

Larry explained that mother's hair started coming out in clumps, so she decided she wanted it all off at one time. Larry talked about the cancer center boutique where mother got her wig and a head scarf for free.

Mother said, "My scarf is purple. Purple is my favorite color." I never knew that.

I had brought a small pink blanket with me that has "God loves you" all over it, because I knew mother might get cold during chemotherapy. My mother asked:

"Can I keep this blanket?"

"No mother. It is only half a blanket. I brought it just for you to use it today."

Mother said okay with a very sad voice.

"Mother, I will bring you one tomorrow that is bigger, and you can keep it."

"Really?"

"Yes, really."

Mother did get cold, so the cancer center staff brought her warm blankets because the half size blanket was not helping much. However, mother made sure it was on top of the rest of the blankets because it was pretty.

The day was long and hard on mother. I rested when mother rested. I still had to take care of myself because I needed to get better so I could return to work. I felt, though, that I was resting better being with my mother. For one, I was out of the house and at a different place. Second, I was helping someone else and it was taking my mind off my own pain. Third, I did it in the name of Forgiveness. I cannot make up for the past and neither can my mother. I was mad at my mother for many years. However, I can change the future and help my mother through her chemotherapy and whatever God has planned for the both of us.

Throughout the day there were several nurses taking care of mother and all of them were really great caretakers. One nurse seemed to come more often and we started talking. While my mother slept, I shared my story with her. I told her she was watching God at work right in front of her, because I never would have been here if it weren't for God.

After a long day, Terry came to pick us both up. It took the nurse, Terry and me to get mother into the truck. But we did it. Mother sat up front with Terry. When we reached the nursing home, it was easier getting mother out of the truck than it was getting her in it.

We took mother to her room, and Terry stayed in the hall while I helped mother change into a hospital gown. Mother said:

> "It is much easier wearing a gown since I got sick and been in the hospital."

> "It is okay with me. It is whatever will make it easy on you."

My mother took off her wig, handed it to me, and told me, "Honey put my wig on that fake head over there." I really wanted to laugh out loud as I thought to myself, *I am glad it wasn't a real head over there*. I did take a double take when mother handed me her wig—my mother was bald-headed!

When I opened the door and invited Terry in the room, I think he was just as surprised at mother's bald head as I was. I asked, "Can I touch your bald head?" Mother said that she did not mind. I don't have a clue why I wanted to touch my mother's head but I did and it felt smooth.

I asked mother if it was okay for Terry to take a picture of the two of us. Mother said yes, so I got behind my mother in her bed while Terry took our picture. Then mother said that she wanted a picture with Terry, as well. I took the photo of her with Terry, then mother said:

"My turn."

"What do you want?"

"I want my picture taken by myself."

Terry and I laughed, and then we took several pictures of her. Mother was proud of her bald head.

Terry said a prayer as we all held hands. His voice was shaky and cracked a little, but he kept on praying! Then, I hugged mother and told her I would see her tomorrow. Mother said, "I love you, too, and don't forget my blanket." I laughed out loud and said, "I won't forget your blanket." Terry said, "Mom I love you." Mother said, "I love you."

As Terry drove me to his house where Steve was going to pick me up, Terry and I talked about how things changed from the first time we heard mother had cancer to now. Because she was getting chemotherapy and radiation, we now had hope that the tumor was shrinking.

When we got to Terry and Jamie's, Steve wasn't there yet. Jamie asked, "Do you want something to eat Darna?" *Darna* is a name Jamie gave me a long time ago, and Jamie is the only one who calls me by that nickname. I told her no. It wasn't long before Steve got there, and we didn't stay long. I was tired and I wanted to go home to get a shower and go to bed.

During the drive home, Steve asked me how it went. I said it went great, considering my mother is getting chemotherapy. I told Steve stories about my conversations with my mother.

When mother wasn't sleeping, the two of us talked about God, miracles, Charlie Rich, and dancing on a hood of a car. I told mother that I don't remember ever dancing on the hood of a car. Mother corrected herself saying:

> "No, I mean when you were little, you danced on top of the kitchen table when Aunt Hazel, Uncle Dick, Cousin Bill and...oh, I can't remember his honey's name.

"Joyce."

"Yes you are right. Bill's honey is Joyce."

I told Steve how much it meant to me just spending time with my mother that day.

Day two of chemotherapy, my alarm went off at 7:00 a.m. I said my prayers even before I got out of bed. I had to make sure I had everything I needed for the day including a blanket for mother.

I took my favorite blanket to mother. The blanket had crosses all over it plus it had her favorite color purple in it. I thought this blanket would be perfect for mother.

Steve dropped me off to the front door of the cancer center. This time I didn't have to tell the receptionist I was here to sit with Shirley Catlett. She just buzzed me through.

When I walked in the room, mother had a purple head scarf on.

"I love your purple scarf, Mother."

"Thanks! Is that my blanket?"

"Yes it is."

I put the blanket over mother and asked if she liked it.

"I love it! It is soooo pretty!"

The nurse came in and told us that it was time to start treatment. Mother said okey-dokey, and then asked the nurse if she like the blanket her daughter had made for her. The nurse said the blanket was very nice. When she left the room I said:

"Mother, I made that blanket a long time ago."

"I know—for me."

I couldn't argue with that! I didn't know way back then that I was making a blanket for my mother.

I thought about S.H.A.C.K. (Serving Hearts Anytime Crisis Knocks.). I was often at Hancock's fabric store or Joann's buying a piece of material without knowing why I was buying it. I believe God knew who the blanket would be going to.

As we were sitting watching old shows on the TV, mother asked:

"How many more days do I have to do this?"

"Mother, this is Thursday. You will have to come back tomorrow and then you will be off two weeks; then on the third week, you will start back up on for three days."

"I am ready to go home."

"I know mother."

"No, I am ready to go home."

I got the feeling mother wasn't talking about the nursing home.

Renae came to pick us up that day. We stopped at Kentucky Fried Chicken on the way back to the nursing home. Mother didn't want to go inside today, so we went through the drive through. We got mother home, helped her to her room, and got her food out for her. I told mother I would see her tomorrow. I said, "I love you." Mother said, "I love you, honey."

The next day was Friday the thirteen and it was mother's last chemotherapy day for two weeks. I didn't have to get up at 7:00 a.m. because they were going to put a pick line in. Larry texted me and told me to come around 10:00 a.m. instead. So I slept in.

Steve dropped me off at 9:50 a.m. Larry and mother were already there. The nurse was having trouble using the pick line that they put in. A nurse practitioner came in and tried to get the line to work, but she was unsuccessful. So, then they tried to get a vein. I stood there watching and listening to mother saying how much it hurts until I had to leave the room. I just could not stand to see my mother in pain like that.

Larry was still in there with mother and the nurses while I just paced back and forth praying that they would get a vein. At one point, I put a finger in each ear as tears streamed down my face. I went to the rest room to wash my face and pull myself back together. I told myself that I was there to help my mother. I was not there to fall apart or have a panic attack. I took five deep breaths and prayed before I walked out the door.

Dear God,

Please be with my mother and help her through the pain. Please be with the nurse practitioner and the nurses as they try to secure a vein to use for mother's treatment, in Jesus' name. Amen.

When I got back to the room, I learned that mother was not going to have treatment today. Larry explained that her veins were bad. Mother would have to come back on Monday to get a new pick line. She was not happy at all about having to get another one of those things put in her arm.

"I don't want that thing in my arm; it hurts."

"I know, but it helps them to give you the treatment."

"I DON'T WANT THAT THING IN MY ARM; IT HURTS!"

"I hear you mother. I will see what I can do about it."

"Okey-dokey. Paul and his family are coming down tomorrow to see me."

"That is great mother."

"I wish I could have all my children all together."

"I know, mother. Maybe one day everyone can come out to Steve's and my house for a cook out."

Mother said okay. As we sat there, we just watched TV and I wondered how in the world I was going to stop them from putting the pick in mother arm.

It didn't take long for Steve to get there because it was past rush hour traffic. Mother asked Steve, "Honey will you take me to the Goodwill store?" Steve told her yes, then checked with me just to make sure. At Goodwill, mother found two pairs of jeans then we went to Kentucky Fried Chicken again on the way back to her nursing home.

As Steve and I drove home, we talked about how funny mother was at the Goodwill store. I was happy my mother had a great day after she left the cancer center.

On Saturday morning, I was sitting on the couch when Larry called.

"Hello."

"Is your husband home?"

"Yes."

At the moment Steve came out of our bedroom. Larry asked, "Can I please talk to him?" I said yes and handed the phone to Steve. As soon as Steve said hello to Larry, I knew. I looked at Steve and said:

"Mother died."

Steve shook his head yes. I don't know how the conversation ended. I know I threw the pencil I had in my hand. Steve came over to sit by me and I cried.

I called Terry but it went to voicemail. I called Jamie and I told her that mother had passed away. Terry was there with her. I let them know that everyone was heading to the nursing home.

I was very quiet on the way to the nursing home. I was thinking about the last three days that mother and I had together. When we got there, all my brothers and one sister was there. Tina was not there yet but she was on her way.

When I saw my brother Paul, I asked:

"Do you know who I am?"

"No Ma'am, I don't."

"I am your youngest sister Darlene."

"It has been a very long time."

"Yes it has."

At first I thought that I would not go into the room to see mother. I remembered what my grandmother looked like when she passed away, and did not want to see my mother like that. I wanted instead to remember the last three days we had together. I did go in the room and I did go over to my mother's bed. Mother looked like she was sleeping. I touched her face and hands while tears ran down my face.

There was a lot of talking and I really wanted to leave. I thought I was going to have a panic attack. Then, I looked down and something caught my eye. I got down on the floor and pulled out a box. It was a clear box with pictures in it. As I looked at the pictures, I knew I was going to use them to make a video for my mother funeral.

After the funeral home came to take mother's body, we all decided to go eat together at Kentucky Fried Chicken. I thought mother would like us eating at her favorite restaurant. When I got out of the car at the restaurant and took a couple of steps, I felt funny. I started swaying. Jamie asked, "When was the last time you ate?" I couldn't remember. I finally was able to walk into the restaurant and sit down while Steve ordered my food.

It was good talking to everyone. I wished it were under different circumstances. As we were all leaving and going are separate ways, Larry let us know that he was meeting with the funeral director tomorrow and invited us to join him. We all hugged each other and went in different directions.

When I got home, I posted on Facebook that my mother had passed away and my family needed prayers. I also asked my family members to post pictures of mother on Facebook. Then, I started right away on making a video of mother's photos. Tomorrow would be a difficult day and I felt so blessed having Steve by my side.

The next day was spent at the funeral home. It was very emotional for all of us. I remembered how mother had said, "I wish I could have all my children together." *I don't think she meant it like this.*

I was trying to get emotionally ready for the funeral and I was thanking God for the last three days I got to spend with mother. I will never forget the "I love you" in the hospital."

After we had our time together with mother, other people started coming in. There were so many people! There were cousins, Aunt Theresa, LaNelle, Kim, and Veronica and Craig from Ohio. Ms. Betty and Linda came, and I introduced them to all of my sisters and brothers.

There were friends from my childhood Sheila and Dawn. There were friends from work Michelle, Pat, Dale, Eddy and Ms. Betty. I was very grateful when my adoptive family—Mom, Dad, Connie and Kim—came and very happy to hug them all. It was great to have members of Crestwood Baptist and Shively Height Baptist Church to support us and pray for us. I cannot name everyone that was there for my siblings and me. I just know that my mother was loved. My siblings, as well, are loved by many people. Even though all of took different paths in life, we all seem to have people who touch our lives or we touch theirs.

I felt so blessed to have my family—Steve, Renae, Michael, Amber, Nathaniel and Nicholas—standing by me and supporting me during this very hard time.

I had the funeral home play *Holy Spirit* by Carrollton. As the song played, it was so powerful. I stood up and gave God the Glory and Praise for the gift he gave to my mother and me in her final days.

GLOSSARY OF CHARACTERS

Some names have been changed to protect identity.

Aunt Gwen	*My mother's sister*
Amber	*Mike's girlfriend*
Aunt Delorse	*My mother 's sister*
Aunt Hazel	*My mother's sister*
Aunt Mildred	*My mother's sister*
Becky	*Stepsister*
Ben	*Tim and Marcie's son*
Ben Malphus	*Director of the Space and Science Center*
Beulah	*Steve's aunt*
Betty Lynn	*Mr. Tucker's Wife*
Blake	*Sunday School member*
Brad Burns	*Youth minister*
Brady	*Kelly's friend*
Camryn	*Michelle's daughter*
Carla	*My mother's friend*
CathyJo Summer	*Licensed Mental Health Counselor*
Charrisa	*Friend*
Cindy	*Sunday School member*
Clint	*First husband*
Connie	*Adoptive sister*

Dale	*Pat's husband*
Dawson	*Kelly's son*
Dean	*Adoptive brother-in-law*
Debbie	*Niece*
Detective Lane	*Officer who investigated my rape case*
Diana	*Co-worker*
Diane	*Adoptive sister-in-law*
Doug	*Adoptive brother-in-law*
Doug	*Sunday School teacher*
Rosie Young	*Principal and mentor*
Eleanor	*Jackie's Sister*
Elmer Stone	*Uncle, father and grandfather*
Esther	*Johnny's mother*
Frances Armstrong	*Steve's mother*
Gary	*Sunday School member and contractor*
Glenn	*Adoptive dad*
Grace	*Stepsister*
Jack	*Steve's uncle*
Jackie	*Wife to Terry Young*
Jamie	*Sister-in-law, married to Terry*
Janice	*Teenage friend*
Jason	*My mother's husband*
Jennifer Carter	*Physics and astronomy teacher from Roman County*
Joann	*Teenage friend*
Joe	*My husband's friend*
Johnny	*Second and third husband*
Joseph	*My husband's boss*

Joyce	*Adoptive mom*
Kathy	*Michelle's friend*
Kelly	*The Amazing Man (ex-boyfriend)*
Kim	*Adoptive sister*
Linda	*Sister*
Lana	*Friend*
Leslie Thomas	*Co-founder of SOAR (Survivors Of Abuse Restored)*
Lindsay Allen	*Co-Anchor for WDRB*
Larry	*Brother*
Luke	*Son of Tim and Marcie*
Mae	*First editor and Sunday School member*
Margo	*Cousin*
Mason	*Stepbrother*
Max	*Johnny's son*
Michele McNeil	*The program coordinator for SpaceTrek*
Michelle	*Friend and co-worker*
Mike	*Son*
Mindy	*Cousin*
Mr. Brown	*College teacher*
Mr. Clark	*College teacher*
Mr. Ryan	*College teacher*
Mr. White	*College teacher*
Ms. Allen	*Missionary from Portland Christian Church*
Ms. Yolanda	*College teacher*
Nathaniel	*Son*
Nicholas	*Son*
Officer Miller	*Police officer who took my statement on the rape*

Pam	*Employee of the rape crisis center*
Pat	*Friend and co-worker*
Paul	*Brother*
Phyllis	*Steve's cousin*
Ray	*Pat and Dale's grandson*
Raymond	*My mother's boyfriend*
Renae	*Daughter*
Rick	*Adoptive brother-in-law*
Rob	*Renae's boyfriend*
Royce	*Steve's step-father*
Sam	*Sunday school member*
Scott	*Johnny's son*
Sharon	*Kelly's sister*
Sheila	*Friend since kindergarten*
Shirley Catlett	*Mother*
Steve	*Fourth and final husband*
Tina	*Sister*
Tara	*Tim and Marcie's daughter*
Terry	*Brother*
Terry Young	*Friend*
Tim	*Cousin, Marcie's husband*
Tonya	*Adoptive sister*
Trish	*Steve's sister*
Uncle Dick	*Aunt Hazel's husband*
Zachary Bruner	*Michelle's son*

SOAR Information

SOAR Ministry – Survivors of Abuse Restored
1940 McDonald Avenue
New Albany, Indiana 47150
812-725-0752
Soarministry.org

SOAR Vision
Soar Ministry is a place where woman who have been sexual abused can find hope and healing through Jesus Christ.

SOAR Mission
Providing Christ-centered recovery for women who have been sexually abused.

Those who hope in the Lord will renew their strength, they will SOAR on wings like eagles, they will run and not grow faint. ~ Isaiah 40:31

Other Resources

Are you under the age of 18 or have you been raped?
Please contact the Rape, Abuse & Incest National
Network (RAINN).
www.rainn.org
24-hour hotline: 800-656-HOPE

Are you a recent victim of domestic violence?
Please call the National Domestic Violence Hotline. They
can help.
www.thehotline.org
Hotline: 800-799-SAFE

Book Recommendation and Reference
Cloud, Henry & Townsend, John. (1994 rev.).
*Boundaries: When to Say Yes, When to Say
No, To Take Control Of Your Life*
Chapter 17 and 22

Made in the USA
San Bernardino, CA
10 February 2017